As a counselor, I've seen the challenges of c
on parents and children alike. What Tamı
book is deal head-on with these challenges wɪ̣ giving loving parents
a different way of relating to each other and their child that's sorely
needed. If you're ready for wise counsel, biblically based tools, and
loads of practical encouragement that will help you relate well to your
co-parent and to bless your child – read this book!

> John Trent, PhD, author of *The Blessing* and president
> of StrongFamilies.com and The Blessing Challenge

As a co-parent, I definitely recommend this book to all parents willing
to work together so their child can lead a well-adjusted life.

> Therese M. Byrne, CLE and meetings director
> of the Tennessee Bar Association

Children need the best their parents have to give. *Co-Parenting Works!*
helps divided parents find common ground for the benefit of their child.
You already love your kid – now give them your best. Read this book.

> Ron L. Deal, author of *The Smart Stepfamily*,
> and founder of www.SmartStepFamilies.com

Tammy realizes the importance of fathers! This is a well-researched
guide that provides excellent advice for those struggling through some
of the most difficult circumstances in life.

> Rick Johnson, founder of www.BetterDads.net and bestselling
> author of *That's My Son, Better Dads – Stronger Sons*
> and *Becoming Your Spouse's Better Half*

Finally! An excellent book that offers wisdom and practical insight into
the complex maze of parenting after divorce! Tammy Daughtry offers a
superb gift of hands-on help for parents, family members, teachers, support group leaders, and church staff who desire to ease a child's pain.

> Laura Petherbridge, author of *When "I Do" Becomes "I Don't"*
> and *The Smart Stepmom*

When marriages fail, children inherit sorrow in proportions for which
their tender souls are unfitted. *Co-Parenting Works!* helps divorced
parents give the love and stability their children need and helps the
wounded retreat from the war.

> Wes Yoder, author of *Bond of Brothers: Connecting
> with Other Men beyond Work* and *Weather and Sports*

We write our wisdom from the trenches of experience. Tammy Daughtry has lived in those trenches when it comes to raising children following divorce. She has done this with grace, purpose, and humor. For families going through the worst chapter of their existence, this book offers help and hope.

Dan Boone, president of Trevecca Nazarene University

I love Tammy Daughtry! And I especially love that she is a beautiful voice equipping this generation for healthy co-parenting after divorce. *Co-Parenting Works!* is a book that has been needed for so long. Let us all learn from Tammy and, for the sake of our children, apply this teaching to our hearts and our lives.

Angela Thomas, bestselling author and speaker

Co-Parenting Works! is both a treasure map and a compass that guides parents navigating the waters of co-parenting past snares and pitfalls in order to discover the beautiful treasure of happy children who will become confident adults. Tammy's work as the co-parenting coach is valuable, necessary, and appreciated.

John Mark "Journey" Johnson, president and CEO
of the YMCA of Middle Tennessee

When divorce has brought your life to the lonely place where you need basic practical advice that works to help you and your children heal and move forward, then you just found it in *Co-Parenting Works!*

Steve Hayes, minister of biblical counseling
for First Baptist Church, Naples, Florida

Excellent ... a much needed resource. Very encouraging and sure to be a great help to those considering co-parenting. Love the personal stories; they make it real!

Robert D. Rabon, president of National Center
for Youth Issues

Tammy is writing about a subject that is near and dear to my heart. I'm the product of a permanent separation, and I can proudly say I got to experience, as a child, what two adults behave like when they realize their differences don't matter and they still have a family that needs parenting. Tammy is doing a service to all of us ... especially co-parents that need to know there is hope for their children.

Joey Elwood, president of Gotee/Mono vs. Stereo Records

Co-Parenting Works!
helping your children thrive after divorce

Tammy Daughtry
Founder of Co-Parenting International

ZONDERVAN®

ZONDERVAN

Co-Parenting Works!
Copyright © 2011 by Tammy G. Daughtry

This title is also available as a Zondervan ebook. Visit www.zondervan.com/ebooks.

This title is also available in a Zondervan audio edition. Visit www.zondervan.fm.

Requests for information should be addressed to:

Zondervan, *Grand Rapids, Michigan 49530*

Library of Congress Cataloging-in-Publication Data

Daughtry, Tammy.
    Co-parenting works! : helping your children thrive after divorce / Tammy
  Daughtry.
       p. cm.
    Includes bibliographical references.
    ISBN 978-0-310-32552-9 (softcover)
    1. Parenting, Part-time. 2. Divorced parents. 3. Joint custody of children.
  4. Children of divorced parents. I. Title.
  HQ755.8.D367 2011
  248.8′4508653—dc22   2010053735

Published in association with Ambassador Literary Agency, Nashville, TN 37205.

Cover design: *Extra Credit Projects*
Cover photography: *Veer*®
Interior design: *Beth Shagene*

Printed in the United States of America

13 14 15 16 17 /DCI/ 22 21 20 19 18 17 16 15 14 13 12 11 10 9 8 7 6 5 4 3 2

With all my love to Angelia Grace …
May you always remember, it's okay to love us both.
I pray your life will be a true example
of God's redemption and proof that co-parenting works!
I love you, Snuggle Bug …

xoxox
♥ Mom

Contents

Foreword

Can this book can change the future for your children? I think so.

It's a fact that the children of divorce struggle to become healthy, productive adults. Many carry the pain of a family breakup into all parts of their adult lives. They often fail at relationships.

Your children don't have to end up that way. *Co-Parenting Works!* equips you with practical strategies to work with your ex-spouse for the benefit of your kids. Whether you have custody of your kids, or your ex does, you can become a better parent if you will apply the strategies Tammy presents in this essential book.

You might be thinking, "You don't know my ex. They would never agree to cooperate at a meaningful level."

Actually, I do know your ex – or at least someone very much like him or her.

Through our DivorceCare support group network, we've helped nearly 700,000 people recover from the ravages of divorce. Many of them are parents. Some were bitter, angry, and uncooperative.

Even those who were hostile and combative, with few exceptions, have a soft spot for their children and deeply care about the well-being of their kids. Their anger might cloud their judgment, leading to mistakes in the way they parent their children, but they still *want* the best for their kids.

Co-Parenting Works! shows you, step-by-step, how to diffuse the tension between you and your ex, and begin the process of working together to raise your children in a healthy way.

If *you* are the angry or distant parent, this book will help you build a bridge back to your children, before it's too late.

And even if you are one of the lucky ones that has a good

relationship with your ex-spouse, you will find lots of wisdom in this book that you can use to directly impact your children — now, and for years to come.

This is not a book written by a head-in-the-clouds academic. Tammy has lived the life of a co-parent, and has done so very successfully. You'll read how she and her former husband worked through the challenges they faced in raising their daughter Angelia. You'll also hear the real-life stories of others who succeeded in making a better life for their kids through co-parenting.

Your children are growing up right before your eyes. It won't be long until they are facing the world as adults. You can't change that.

You can, however, transform their emotional and spiritual health by applying the principles you will learn in *Co-Parenting Works!* The stakes are enormous. The time to act is now.

Steve Grissom
Founder, DivorceCare/Single & Parenting
www.divorcecare.org
www.singleandparenting.org

Finding Your Heart
in Love and War

Any Christmas Eve at 6:00 p.m. during Leslie's childhood: sitting in the back seat of her mom's car in the parking lot of the 7 – 11, weeping in grief and frustration to the sound of her parents' enraged shouts at each other outside the car. Police sirens. Flashing red-and-blue lights. The sound of a policeman trying to calm her parents down, telling them he doesn't want to run them in on Christmas Eve, but if they don't stop disturbing the peace—

What peace?

Leslie would clutch her favorite teddy bear to her face, trying to shut it all out, make it go away ...

Leslie's parents, though they divorced when she was a baby, continued their personal war all through her growing-up years. When she looks back at childhood, the painful memories surface first: the arguing, the fighting over child support and who would pay for summer camp, the guilt trips each laid on her about spending too much time with the other parent, the heartache of driving away with her father while her mother wept because she was going to spend a holiday away.

Christmas was split down the middle at 6:00 p.m. on Christmas Eve, the handoff time to whichever parent had Leslie for Christmas Day that year. Parking lots were the neutral handoff spot where pillows, suitcases, teddy bears, and one very nervous little girl would be transferred from one car to another. Her parents couldn't manage even that much without taking the opportunity to vent their rage at each other. The sad truth is that the two people Leslie loved the most were good at only one thing—putting her in the middle and trying to make her choose who she loved the most. And because of that, Leslie's memories of childhood are memories of pain and crisis, chaos and confusion, anger and resentment.

Did Leslie's parents want to inflict pain and chaos and frustration on her life? Of course not – they loved her just as she loved them. Why then did they make her childhood so unpleasant?

I believe they didn't know how to handle the situation any better. They had no constructive and productive models for being the divorced co-parents of a sensitive and trusting child. How I wish someone had given them a road map to co-parenting – to working together, even though they were divorced, out of mutual love for the child they had brought into the world. How I wish someone could have helped them anticipate the monumental moments of Leslie's life – graduations, recitals, prom – so they could have all enjoyed those occasions together instead of trying to avoid the countless emotional landmines. How I wish a book or seminar had been available to help them figure out how to communicate with each other, difficult though it may have sometimes been, in the effort to help their little girl thrive. How I wish someone had explained to them that it's not about tearing down the other parent – it's about building up the child.

This book is that road map. These stories are the directional signs. The mistakes and successes of others are the guardrails for the next generation of co-parents to follow.

As a parent who has now been co-parenting for ten years – and as someone who, like Leslie, grew up under divorced, warring parents – I have found it is possible to move beyond anger and pain to a positive and cooperative attitude in co-parenting. It is possible to work together, for the sake of the child. It is possible to have a strong parenting partnership even though you didn't have a strong marriage, and to shield children from the ongoing hurts caused by divorce. Your child does not have to be another negative statistic. Your child can thrive, excel, adjust, and live life fully – in mom's house, and also in dad's.

Is co-parenting after divorce easy? No. Does positive co-parenting come naturally? No. Cooperating with the person with whom you had irreconcilable differences requires concentrated effort from both parties. And a whole lot of God-given grace.

Healthy co-parenting is critical for the sake and safety of your children, and can break the cycle of divorce and promote marriage and family in the future.

Are your kids worth the effort? You decide.

For years I have been hosting seminars that teach the principles and techniques of co-parenting. Do those principles work? Here are a few comments from people who've taken my co-parenting seminars:

> *"I don't want to pass the torch of brokenness to my kids. I sensed hope for them."*
>
> *"I learned that my son needs to celebrate his dad, too. I can't be both parents."*
>
> *"I realized I am doing many things right, but I learned 100 more ideas I never knew to do!"*
>
> *"I want to be a stable parent and this seminar showed me I am being insecure and childish. I need to get healthy so I can be a better model to my daughter."*
>
> *"I did not know how much damage I was doing when I talked bad about their dad."*
>
> *"Immediately after the co-parenting seminar I went to my son's soccer game. For the first time in six years, I sat on the same side of the field as my ex-wife. I realized that part of co-parenting is getting out of my own comfort zone so my son won't feel so divided. He came off the field and was able to high-five us both instead of having to choose which parent to go see first. I had no idea how much that was hurting him all those years. I have to admit, I was uncomfortable sitting on the same side as my ex but I had to remember — it's not about me, it's about my son!"*
>
> *"After hearing about the importance of photos I asked my ex-husband if I could take a photo of him and our two children. I went to Walgreen's and printed out one copy for my son's room and one for my daughter's*

*room. They each now have an area in their rooms to put important
things that remind them of their dad. I am doing that for their good, so
the holes in their hearts will be much smaller in the future."*

I have seen lives changed by those seminars. I have seen families, even though they were no longer intact, regain wholeness and
health, so that the children of divorce could thrive.

The principles and techniques from that seminar are distilled
into this book. The information and advice you need to navigate
the co-parenting path, and do it well, is here, in your hands. You
will hear the comments of co-parents about their obstacles and
their efforts to find solutions. You will hear from adult children of
divorce about what their parents did right—and what they wish
their parents had done differently. You will also hear from young
children currently being raised between two homes—and you will
learn from their hurts and their happiness.

Friends, with strength and with a focus on your children's
heart, you *can* become an amazing co-parenting team with your
former spouse—including when stepparents come into the picture.
I know that you love your children, or you wouldn't have picked
up this book. Let that love motivate you to do whatever it takes to
facilitate a healthy childhood for your children. Determine to focus
fully on what is best for your children's future. Be the one who
leads the way with quiet strength that is more concerned about
your children's heart and your children's future than about who is
to blame for the past.

Your children were given to you on purpose! Out of the millions of parents on the planet, God gave them to you. And when he
did, he presented you with an amazing job. Your influence on your
children now is forming a family legacy that will live on long after
you are gone. What will your kids say as they reflect on *their* childhood? Will they remember smiles and high fives at their athletic
events—or unspoken hostility and cold wars? Will they remember
destructive anger—or that you chose peace? Will they remember
a happy good-bye at their handoff time to the other parent, or will
they remember tears, insecurity, and sadness?

The answers to those questions lie in the choices that you make and in the way you and your ex conduct yourselves as co-parents.

Your ability to co-parent well is *the* most critical aspect of life after divorce for your children. It is the foundation to all of the details lived out in your everyday lives. Having lived it for several years now, I know firsthand that co-parenting is not easy; but I also know that it is worth every ounce of effort—because it is through that effort that our children can have the healthiest foundation on which to build their futures.

CHAPTER 1

Getting Started in Co-Parenting

Though you have made me see troubles,
many and bitter, you will restore my life again;
from the depths of the earth you will again bring me up.
You will increase my honor and comfort me once again.

PSALM 71:20-21

Weeping may remain for a night,
but rejoicing comes in the morning.

PSALM 30:5

I sat at my kitchen table, crying. I stared through my tears at the blurry neighborhood outside. "God, do you even see me sitting here right now?" I prayed. "Do you see my tears? Do you know how much I'm hurting? Do you sense how terrified I am about the future? I'm a single parent now! How can I raise a child alone? How will I pay the bills? Where will I live? How will I ever face the judgment of the people around me, people I love, who judge us because we're getting divorced? I *know* you hate divorce. I know you hate what it does to your children. I know you hate what it will do to my child ..."

I wiped my eyes with a tissue. The details of my life on that morning seemed like a knotted, tangled mess that I couldn't unravel, couldn't make sense of.

I begin this story here, at this memory of a place of pain in my life, because although I have journeyed years beyond those overwhelming moments and the haunting questions, I will *never* forget them. I will never forget how I felt during those dark days: as if I were in a thick fog. I had no idea what was on the other side of that fog, or even when I would get through it. My past was a sea of regrets, and I was completely disillusioned about the future.

My emotions after the divorce were intense and painful – hard for even me to understand, and even harder to describe to my friends. Their words of "encouragement" sometimes seemed to be half judgment and condemnation, as if they couldn't speak to me without first making clear where they stood on the issue of divorce. Their unasked questions about why and who was to blame made every conversation awkward and uncomfortable.

I thought it odd at the time that they felt the need to express their moral objection to divorce. Did they really think anyone was more uncomfortable with the idea of divorce than I was at that time? I was experiencing firsthand the pain divorce caused! Watching my marriage deteriorate and crumble was not what I dreamed about as a child. I'm sure none of us grew up imagining we would find our princess or prince charming, get married (in a castle), have babies – and then end up divorced.

Success isn't measured by the things you achieve, but by the obstacles you overcome.
ETHAN HAWKE

That's not the "happily ever after" we imagined. Our wedding day with rice and flowers and kisses wasn't supposed to lead to a war that resulted in your children growing up in two separate houses, or in only one with another parent they never see.

Not all of us down the path of divorce have come to the threshold of co-parenting. To many readers, this picture of the newly divorced, grieving mother may seem beside the point. Perhaps you've never been married, and are looking for ways to keep your children's other biological parent involved in their life. Perhaps you lost a spouse or partner to illness or war or an accident, and you're looking for guidance in managing other relatives, perhaps grandparents, who want to be involved in your children's lives. In any of these cases, our circumstances are similar: you're now a single parent, and another caregiver or parent has a presence in your children's life; you're looking for ways to facilitate that presence in a way that's fair and helpful for all parties.

That's what we hope to guide in this book. Not so much for your sake, although in the end you'll find parenting to be better with a committed co-parent. And not so much for your co-parent's sake, although, in the end, he or she will be glad to be involved in raising and loving that precious child. We do all of this for the sake of the children we love. Keep that in mind; when things gets tough, as it will at times, you'll remember why it's worth it.

Whatever circumstances set you on this course—especially if you're just beginning and your heart is hurting so badly that the word *heartache* makes sense to you for the first time—in this book you have found a place of grace. No one is judging you here, and you share this experience with many others. Welcome.

One Heart, Two Homes

Before your divorce, even though one parent may have assumed most child-rearing duties, your children relied on both of you to bring stability and security to their world. The things about your spouse, now ex-spouse, that drove you crazy were not lost on your kids either, but kids have a wonderful and immediate forgiveness response. And they have that response because they sensed an important and crucial truth: they need both of you. I have almost never heard of young children who wanted their parents to divorce. For the vast majority of children, their parents' divorce was that unthinkable disaster that would bring their whole world crashing into incurable disaster. It was the monster under the bed.

As a result, kids of divorce can't imagine a world in which both parents won't continue to love them and be involved in their lives. That would be the realization of their worst fears.

Children of divorce have one heart, but they live in two homes. What co-parents do to protect their children's hearts is the key to an enjoyable childhood and healthy upbringing for them—even when they have two families, two bedrooms, and two very different lives. Creating a co-parenting team with your ex, working together for the sake of your children, will reap rewards for your children that are far more valuable than anything tangible you could give them.

It's not about you; it's about your kids.

It's not about the past; it's about your kids' future.

For their long-term well-being, your kids need you to take the sometimes difficult step of creating a co-parenting team with your ex. Right now you may have serious doubts that such a thing could ever be; and even if the two of you agreed to do it, you have doubts about how well it would work. That's what we'll be discussing in the rest of this book. I'll try to anticipate and deal with each question and doubt you have—which are probably the same ones the participants in my seminars raise over and over again.

The End Adult Matters Most

If I'm your co-parenting coach, then like any good coach I want to give you an overview of where we're going and what our goals are. Even if all you do is just read through this book, you'll still pick up some helpful takeaways. By also digesting and implementing these ideas, you can radically change your life and the lives of your children, now and far into the future—which means you'll also be affecting the lives of your unborn grandchildren. Quite a return on your investment of time and effort!

What will you accomplish? With sincere commitment to excellent co-parenting, you will be able to:

- Communicate with your co-parent calmly, with purpose and clarity.

- Intentionally schedule time with your co-parent to discuss important issues related to your child—and, yes, even find solutions.

- Focus on the positive aspects of giving your children the freedom to love both parents.

- Attend—along with your co-parent and any stepparents—your children's school functions, athletic events, and all extra-curricular events with peace and anticipated enjoyment.

- Speak words of life and hope to your children about their other parent.

- Celebrate the love and the time your children share with their other parent.

- Exercise emotional maturity when something hurtful happens.

- Choose to leave some things unsaid for the best interest of your children.

- *Co-parent forward* — make co-parenting decisions today that will affect your children positively five years and ten years from now.

- Be a positive "first filter" to all outside influences to your children's lives.

- Plan ahead what you will do when your children are away during holidays — to avoid loneliness and depression. Create a "fun plan" for yourself.

- Create a support system to help you process difficulties with your co-parent.

- Anticipate your children's monumental moments in life and create a game plan that allows all family members — from both sides of your children's family — to participate amiably and enjoyably.

- Prepare for your children's adulthood: graduations, weddings, and future grandchildren.

- Understand fully what is at stake — the heart of your children and *their* future.

- Begin with the end in mind: What will your children say twenty years from now? What will their lives be like, and how will your decisions today affect that future?

- Commit to a positive co-parenting *TEAMM mentality* — because, as the TEAMM acronym denotes: **The End Adult Matters Most**!

Memories …

Before we dive into the rest of the book, I want you to write down your top childhood memories — good, bad, or otherwise. Don't worry about being exhaustive; this isn't a test. No pressure. Just write down the first memories that come to mind. After all, there's a reason they're the first memories you think of. Spend a few minutes to reflect, and be honest, even if some of these memories are painful. If, in fact, some of them are so painful you don't want to commit them to writing here, just use code words that only you would understand—the day, or the place, or some detail that you connect with the event.

_____

_____

_____

_____

_____

_____

_____

Why did I ask you to complete this exercise, even though it may, for some of you, have dredged up unpleasant thoughts? Two reasons. First, understanding your past can strengthen your future. You may have sad memories of hurts inflicted upon you by people you love. Unresolved issues may still fill you with anger or sadness. On the other hand, many memories probably make you smile, even laugh out loud. You may feel pride and a sense of accomplishment to have been part of your family's legacy, a legacy that still lives on inside of you.

When I look back, some of my best memories connect me to my grandparents, both the Gallegos and Grasmick families. I am grateful to be an extension of those individuals—a fun mix of German and Spanish influences, beliefs, values, and family traditions. I still get choked up at the sound of upbeat Spanish music as I remember the weddings and "wedding marches" of our family heritage, and how I loved to dance across the floor with my Grandpa Gallegos. These days, when I smell coffee early in the morning, I think of my Grasmick grandparents. As a child, I would roll over in the morning at first awakening, hearing the coffee percolate, and know that they were up and waiting for me. How I wish I could still wander, sleepy-eyed, to their kitchen table and read the Rocky Ford newspaper and plan for the Saturday yard sales.

These memories linger, and I am so grateful for them. I believe that God knew, out of the millions of parents he could have given me to, that I was to belong to these two families, and for that I thank him.

> It takes a whole nation to raise this generation.
>
> KIRK FRANKLIN

This brings us to my second reason for asking you to list your strongest memories: Your children are right now, as we speak, forming the memories that, good or bad, will make up their future list of "strongest memories." And they've already had both kinds — the good ones that will make them smile or laugh some future day, as well as the ones that will bring tears to their eyes.

You can't protect them from having some sad or painful memories — life deals those out to us whether we want them or not. But you can work with your ex-spouse to keep the negative memories to a minimum and to intentionally create occasions for your children that will foster happy memories, the kind they'll someday be as grateful for as I am of my memories of my Gallegos and Grasmick grandparents.

All of this is within your power — yours, and your co-parent's.

The Exercises

You'll find exercises like the recounting of memories you just did scattered through the book — not in every chapter, but often. Some of you tend to skip over exercises like these when you find them in books. I encourage you to resist skipping the exercises. They're here for a reason. You'll get much more out of the book, I assure you, if you complete these exercises. Take the initiative, and the minute or two it will take to do the work each time. You'll improve your ability to cope with the challenging situation you face, and because of that, your kids and your grandkids will benefit. Your work environment will benefit. Your own heart and soul will benefit. It's one thing to skim through a book like this, but it can become something entirely different when you commit to internalizing what you've learned.

I have been in your shoes. I'm *still* in them, since I will forever be a co-parent with my daughter's dad, and I will forever have complexities to process — even twenty years from now. I want you to get strong and healthy, and I want you to avoid every mistake humanly possible so that your children will have the very best YOU — and the very best life!

To ensure that — do the work. Fill in the blanks.

Meet the Cast

Throughout this book, I'll be sharing stories with you from the lives of people who've grown up in homes split by divorce — some from homes in which parents co-parented wisely, and some in which their parents made no attempt to co-parent cooperatively at all. We'll also hear from people engaged, as you are, in the task of co-parenting. As you consider the consequences of your own choices, it's helpful to hear how similar choices have affected the lives of others. I've changed the names of those people, of course, so they didn't have to worry about how their honest comments might hurt the feelings of their loved ones. I want you to meet the cast.

Joey is an adult child of divorce. He's married now, with kids himself, but he remembers the years after his own parents' divorce. He was twelve when it happened, just entering those difficult teenage years; and the pain of knowing he was not going to be able to grow up with both of his parents around him all the time was paralyzing. His grades dipped markedly that first year and stayed low the next. At first, he was told that he'd be spending every other weekend with his dad, and he considered it something to look forward to; but those weekends rarely materialized. It seemed to Joey that his mom came up with every excuse imaginable why Joey couldn't go with his dad on those weekends, and Joey's hopes that his dad would fight for him were in vain. Eventually Joey saw his dad only on holidays and for a week or so in the summer. He grew up grieving the loss of the relationship with his father.

Tina's parents divorced when she was a baby, so she never knew her parents as a couple, only as the two people she loved most. She remembers that throughout her childhood, they still argued heatedly. An only child, she cried herself to sleep many nights. Today, she's in her early thirties and has never wanted to get married. "Why take the risk?" she says. She has internalized all the negativity she heard from her parents about each other, and the effects of that on her life are many. For instance, she usually dates men who are emotionally abusive or just absent, because she has never seen a healthy example of love. She also has a hard time forgiving others for any type of offense, because the closest example she had for handling wrongs was her mom, who stayed mad indefinitely about every wrong done to her. Tina tries to let go of her past, but it seems to cling to her. She is truly lonely – but she dreads the idea of marriage because her parents would both be in the same room. That has never gone well.

Even though **Leslie's** parents divorced when she was five, she has vivid memories of them together. Every encounter was a fight that ended in tears. Her mom, always chasing a dream, moved almost every year. Her dad was a workaholic whose other major priority was drinking. Leslie was with him every other weekend, but emotionally he never seemed to connect. Her mom remarried and re-divorced three more times. Her dad never remarried, but always had a girlfriend around when Leslie was with him. Leslie remembers her dad's girlfriends as a revolving door – she never knew, when she went to her dad's house, whether she'd meet the one from last visit or a new one. Leslie numbed out as a teen. By fifteen, she was drinking and having sex in an attempt to feel some level of love. Currently in college, she has many concerns about the future. Her only sense of home comes from her grandparents; her mom and dad have transient lifestyles – physically, relationally, and emotionally. Leslie has been sexually active with at least nine people. She is twenty-one.

Steve, twice divorced, has three kids from those two marriages and has struggled unsuccessfully to establish positive and productive co-parenting relationships with his ex-wives. Now in his third marriage, he's relieved that his older kids are reaching adulthood so that he can relate to them without the interference of an uncooperative ex, but worries about how family events such as weddings will go. His third marriage has been a revelation to him; he'd never known what a happy, mutually satisfying and supportive marriage felt like. Now he does.

Levi was raised in a traditional Christian home. He was married for ten years. He and his former wife have two daughters who were very young when their mom moved away, leaving the girls to live with their father. Against all odds, Levi provided a strong, stable home for his girls. For several years after her departure, the girls didn't see their mother very often, and Levi was their full-time and only day-to-day parent. He eventually moved closer to his ex, to allow them to see their mother more often. Since then, things have settled into an active co-parenting relationship. Levi has never tried to use her "absent" years against his ex, nor has he spoken negatively about her to his daughters. In this, he's motivated not by his sense of what is fair or by what the courts said he had to do. He's simply trying to choose what is best for his children, and he believes what is best for them is having two strong, stable, loving parents.

Bruce and his four brothers were raised by a single mom after being abandoned by their father. Defying all the statistics for children after divorce, he's been happily married for over thirty-five years. He enjoys his children and grandchildren, and in his professional life, he has made a huge impact on the world through the Christian music industry. His mother, who freely sought help from church and family during her single parenthood, never remarried —but she raised five strong, godly men who are all being used in Christian service around the globe.

And don't forget my family, who make frequent appearances on these pages. **Angelia**, my daughter, is eleven years old as I'm writing this. Her father and I divorced when Angelia was two. About seven years ago, he remarried, and together they're a blended family of six, counting Angelia.

I was a single mom for eight years. Then I met **Jay**, who had lost his wife in a car accident four-and-a-half years ago. When we married, I was blessed to have the opportunity to love and care for three more children: **Amanda**, **Jenna**, and **Jaron**. We, too, are a blended family of six.

Where Are We Going?

Where do we go next? Where is this book taking us?

The next chapter begins Part 1: "Becoming a Stable and Effective Co-Parent." The chapters in that section analyze how it came to this—the road that has led you to co-parenting, and what steps you should take to ensure your own psychological health for dealing with the sometimes challenging task of co-parenting. We'll talk about the support team you already have, perhaps without realizing it, and the additional support you can enlist. And we'll consider how to pursue your own stability so that you're not approaching co-parenting with an empty tank, but rather from a position of strength.

Part 2 reminds you that "It's Not About You—It's About the Kids." We'll look at the effects of divorce on children. Some of them may surprise you. We'll also look at the dynamics of the post-divorce world for kids, and at their desperate need to be able to love, and spend time with, *both* of their parents.

Then comes what for many of you will be the hard part: Part 3, "Creating a Co-Parenting Team." We'll look at several different models for co-parenting—some of them effective, some not. We'll talk about how to broach the subject with your ex, and about the importance of co-parenting meetings to discuss issues with the kids — including how to conduct the meetings and what to cover. We'll also look at the tough issue of creating consistent standards on such things as discipline in both homes, and how to handle the eventual inclusion of stepparents on that team.

What happens when your ex is uncooperative, or other family members are creating problems, or other complications arise? Every co-parenting team faces obstacles, and they're the subject of Part 4. Most of those obstacles are surmountable. What happens when they're not — when your ex absolutely refuses to join a co-parenting effort, refuses to refrain from saying things or taking actions that hurt the kids, or simply disappears? We cover those concerns in Part 5.

Eventually, one or both members of your co-parenting team will move on — begin dating again, and perhaps remarry. That's Part 6.

And Part 7 looks even further into the future: we'll look again at creating great life memories, and at the ways your words and actions now will affect your kids' adult lives — as well as at the dynamics of co-parenting for *life*, not just while the kids are young.

I hope those seven parts and twenty-one chapters will cover adequately the issues and opportunities you'll face in building and operating your co-parenting team. If not, I provide lists of additional resources in an appendix, with more information on my website, www.CoParentingInternational.com, where you can also find video segments for each part of the book.

Ready for Part 1?

PART ONE

Becoming a Stable and Effective Co-Parent

CHAPTER 2

How on Earth
Did It Come to This?

A pioneer by circumstances, not by choice ...
JOHN TRENT, *Pictures Your Heart Remembers*

Steve's story is typical of many of us: "I grew up in a stable Christian home. My parents are still married, in fact. We attended church regularly, and everything I heard, both at home and at church, told me that marriage was 'till death do you part.' My bride and I, when I married, had never really known any couples who had serious marital difficulties — or who didn't hide them well. So imagine our surprise — and sense of guilt — when our first year of marriage was filled with tension and anger and unproductive, fruitless argument. We wondered what was wrong with us, that we should have such problems when, as far as we knew, no one else did.

"We survived that year. But the marriage was never really happy, and tension was never far below the surface. After ten years and two kids, my wife filed for divorce.

"I wasn't sure I'd ever marry again; but a couple of years later, I met a sweet woman I thought I could trust and married a second time. All of our five combined kids took part in the ceremony with us.

"To my amazement, the first year of this marriage wasn't any easier than the first year of the first marriage had been. We were both older, wiser, and I thought more reasonable than in my first marriage — so why wasn't it working better? Was it just me? Was there something about me that made wives desperately unhappy?

"What a sense of failure and guilt and frustration I felt several years later when my second wife, like the first, filed for divorce. The daughter the two of us had brought into the world, like the kids from my first marriage, was now fated to grow up the child of divorce. All I'd ever wanted was to be the father and husband in a stable and loving home that honored God and lived selflessly for each other and for him. Instead, I was now twice-divorced with kids living uneasily between two homes.

"How on earth had it come to this?"

Can you relate?

Even though Steve's story may be somewhat different from your own, you can undoubtedly relate to his sense of guilt and failure. Steve, like many of us, knew the statistics about children of divorce—how much more likely they were, for instance, to do poorly in school and to engage in at-risk behavior, and how much less likely they were to make a success of their own marriages. He worried what all of this meant for his children—and when his teenaged daughter ran into substance abuse issues, he was sure the predictions implied in the statistics were proving true.

The negative statistics involving the children of divorce aren't predictions. Not by any means. They're simply the measurement of how poorly many—not all!—parents have responded to the needs of children of divorce. You have it within your power to turn that situation completely around through wise parenting—and by diligently collaborating with your own ex-spouse in the one enterprise the two of you may be able to agree on: the wise and caring parenting of your own children, the children you both love.

But first we need to understand what's happening. Most of you picked up this book because you're a divorced parent. It's crucial, then, that we understand some of the dynamics of divorce.

This is not a book on divorce recovery, although I suggest you find that too. This is a book on co-parenting children. So let's look at some of the dynamics of divorce that affect your ability to parent your own kids.

The Post-Divorce Timeline

Psychologist and researcher into issues of divorce Mavis Hetherington of the University of Virginia has found, in her pioneering research into the lives of over 1,400 families, that the first year after divorce is the hardest adjustment period. In fact, the stress and difficulty in adjustment is at its peak at the end of year one.[1] On average, the end of the first twelve months after a divorce hits right at the peak of the bell curve – its highest point of pain and difficulty. That's when most divorced people find the going the hardest – emotionally, financially, and just in the overall sense that your life is out of sync.

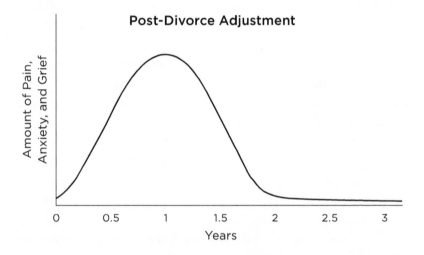

Thankfully, Hetherington also concludes that by the end of year two, most parents are back to a place of functional stability and doing as well as they were before the divorce. If your experience is like that of most people, you can predict and plan on the first year being hard, but it's reasonable to hope that by the end of year two, you'll be much more adjusted.

The pain and angst and difficulty you feel during year one won't have the same intensity throughout, either, and your ability to adjust will increase. Still, it's normal and predictable to feel overwhelmed, angry, and even hopeless at times during the first year. Don't beat yourself up for your negative feelings; they're normal. Dig in and face them. Look them in the eye and determine that they will not beat you. When you realize this difficult time won't last forever, that your life will get better someday, you can hang on. Challenges will come, but you won't be defeated.

The children that God has blessed you with are worth every effort that a tired parent puts into loving and supporting them during this tough time – the kisses at bedtime and the hugs before school, the smiles at athletic events and the extra driving for the music lessons are all part of staying strong for the children.

Just starting your post-divorce journey? Mark your calendar for one year from the start of your divorce, one so you can anticipate difficulty, and then for two, to remind yourself it won't always hurt the way it does today. You'll get over the hump of the curve, and from that point on, you'll keep gaining emotional stability.

Self Care

Taken any flights on commercial airlines lately? I've taken so many over the years that, like many travelers, I no longer listen to the safety instructions the flight attendants give as you wait on the runway for takeoff. I can practically quote the spiel word for word: "In the unlikely event of a loss in cabin pressure, oxygen masks will descend from the console above you. Place one firmly over your nose and mouth. If you are traveling with an infant or small child, put on your own oxygen mask first before placing one on your child."

What? Take care of your own safety first *before* taking care of your child? It goes against the grain for nearly every parent! But one doesn't have to think about it very long to understand why. If you start to put the mask on your child first, and then pass out from lack of oxygen because you aren't wearing a mask yourself, you could both die. But if you put your own mask on first, you won't pass out, and you'll be able to place the mask on your child successfully. You'll both live – but only because you made sure your own needs were taken care of so that you'd be strong and able to take care of your child.

Recovery from divorce is something like that. You're painfully conscious of your children's needs, and you desperately want to fix them; but don't ignore your own need for healing and for help. If you don't take care of yourself in this tough, vulnerable period, you may not be in any shape to take care of your children's needs.

A great resource to help you assess and meet those needs of your own, and one that was life-giving for me when I was going through my divorce, is DivorceCare. I was aware of it before my divorce only because I had seen the signs advertising the meetings, but I didn't know much about it. DivorceCare is a series of weekly classes – thirteen weeks' worth – guiding divorced people through the process of divorce recovery and providing encouragement and camaraderie at a time when people desperately need it.

I have to laugh at myself. I was too embarrassed to attend the class at my church where everyone knew me, so I went to the DivorceCare website (www.divorcecare.com/findagroup) and put in my zip code. At least a dozen other places in the area were offering the class. I called a couple until I found the right fit for me – a class that met one night a week.

In those classes, in that group, I found the strength to keep going. Even though I'm an extrovert (on steroids), I can't say that I was excited to walk into that room the first day – in fact I was nervous. But I sucked it up and went in. After that, it was very easy to go back week after week. What I found in that class were other people just like me, people who were recovering from an unpleasant, often unwanted divorce. Although we all had different life stories, we had a common cause. We were hurting and we wanted to heal. We were broken but we wanted to be restored. We had questions, many still unanswered, but we found hope in the journey together.

Even if you've already been divorced for years, I recommend that you find a DivorceCare class or other divorce recovery program in your community and sign up. You'll find support as you navigate the troubling waters of lost relationship. If you're just recently separated and think you can't add one more thing to your plate, find something you can take *off* your plate for the next few weeks and add this instead.

I learned, in DivorceCare, that my erratic emotions and fears were normal. I learned that my feelings of being exhausted and overwhelmed were to be expected. I learned that it was healthy to get angry and then to process that anger. I learned that I was already making normal progress through my grief and loneliness. I was given tools to help guide my thinking about dating and sexuality after divorce. I was able to learn from other people's mistakes, lessening the likelihood that I would make those same mistakes myself. Because I was with a group of vulnerable people who were in the same boat I was in, I could let my guard down and not try to hide my distress, my loneliness, my anxiety — and it was okay. *I* was okay! Even though I might not see evidence of it every day, I was healing. Discovering these things gave me hope.

Becoming a single parent was like re-creating and redefining myself. I had been part of a married couple. I had been a married parent. Now I had to figure out who I was on my own. I had to figure out what I liked to eat for dinner with Angelia — and what to eat without Angelia. I had to plan for holidays and create new traditions. I had to decide what color to paint the walls in the little rented duplex I moved into. I had to decide whether to sit in front of a TV at night and mindlessly stare at the screen or to go to bed and get the rest my body needed. I had to decide if I was going to exercise or just sit on the couch and be sad.

For the very first time in my whole life, I was living alone. For an extrovert, that isn't fun. Growing up, I had lived with my mom and visited my dad. In college, I always had roommates in the dorms. After graduation, starting my career, I would share apartments and townhouses with roommates. Then I got married. Now I was thirty-two, and on the nights Angelia was with her dad, I was facing an empty house for the first time, figuring out how to make life work all alone. Many lonely nights I just sat on my couch and cried. Many lonely Saturday mornings I woke up only to roll over and try to sleep again so I wouldn't notice how quiet the house was.

You adjust to the post-divorce life gradually. Little by little, I learned to walk it out – to make my day-to-day life work. And in that slow, sometimes frustrating slog, my DivorceCare class one night a week became a true highlight. I looked forward to it. I often heard new insights from other class attendees when we had our small group discussion time. I also remember being affirmed by the video presenters, who frequently reminded me that I was not alone – that millions of other divorced parents like me had to find their way one step at a time – and that I could learn from those who had walked that path before me. When I listened to the real-life stories of my classmates, I was reminded that my situation wasn't as tragic as it sometimes felt. I could even be thankful for my own circumstances; many others were in situations so much worse.

I learned much about how to co-parent Angelia. I learned that if I took great care of myself and my emotional needs, and if I found healthy ways to walk the road before me, I was also benefiting my daughter. I learned that if my ex-spouse and I could find ways to work through the complications of co-parenting without putting Angelia in the middle, then even though our daughter would always have two homes, the bridge between them would be stable and steady.

Simply put, I found encouragement and wisdom from the other divorced friends I found in DivorceCare. We walked through a difficult time together, and we helped each other become healthier and more stable in the process.

Throughout this book, you'll find other suggestions to help in the all-important task of self-care.

CHAPTER 3

You Are Not Alone — Even If It Sometimes Feels Like It

*My saddest memories of Christmas
were seeing my mom cry when I left with my dad.*
JOEY, age 41

Like many children of divorce, Joey grew up with a divided Christmas. He remembers how he hated to see his mom fall apart when he was leaving to see his dad: "I never felt like she was going to be okay while I was gone. Her tears would make me feel like I had to make her happy and that it was my fault she was sad. I never left feeling I could go and have fun with my dad; I actually felt guilty. I always felt I should go back to take care of my mom and make sure she was okay.

"As early as age nine, I remember thinking I had to call my mom every day I was with my dad, just to see if she was all right. I remember her crying over the phone about how much she missed me. I hated to hear that, because it made me feel guilty—so worried about her that I couldn't have fun with my dad's family.

"Looking back, I wish someone had told my mom to pull herself together and not place that kind of pressure on me. Whether she was aware of it or not, she was making me responsible for her happiness. I know my mom had friends; I wish she had made some plans with them, and then told me as I was leaving about the fun things she was going to do with them, or that she was going to go visit someone while I was away. The mental image of her sitting at home, crying, alone and sad caused enough guilt to last more than my lifetime."

It's important for your kids, and it's important for you, that you not take the approach to handling your "alone-ness" that Joey's mother did. Your kids are not responsible for you—it's the other way around. To keep from placing an undue burden on their shoulders, you need to make sure that the image they have of you when they're with their other parent is not of you "sitting at home, crying, alone and sad."

You Are Not Alone

First, regardless of how you feel at the moment, and regardless of how you felt last night when you cried yourself to sleep, know that you are *not* alone. The pain you feel is a normal part of the process, and thousands of single parents are feeling it every day. Here's a message you will hear over and over again in this book—until you begin to believe it: What seems to you now like an everlasting agony, a sorrow that will never go away, a cloud that will never disappear—I promise you, it will not hurt forever as it hurts today. The darkness is temporary.

You are not alone because God walks with you

Some days we simply can't see our way clear for even one step ahead. At those times we must trust God to lead us through, knowing he sees beyond today. You are not alone—because God walks with you, as he did with David the psalmist, through the valley of the shadow of death.

I remember the feeling that I was grasping for something to hold onto as the pieces of my life crumbled all around. Sometimes that collapse happens in one single shocking moment—a spouse walks in and announces that he or she is leaving, or you discover an affair. Sometimes the process takes years, as a marriage dies a long, hard, slow, agonizing death. The details are unique to each person's journey, yet the crumbling may feel very much the same to all of us. All that we dreamed of and all that we hoped for seems to be falling apart, and we can do absolutely nothing to hold it together. The plans we had for lifelong love and a fiftieth wedding anniversary begin to fade into what feels like the black abyss of nothingness. The annual holidays we tried to make perfect and full of meaningful tradition now have to be completely redefined, and we know they will never be the same. All that we'd hoped for and all that we'd dreamed of must now be sorted through, divided in half, and moved to separate households.

In the midst of that madness, I found one solid truth to hold onto: God hates divorce, but he *loves* the people who go through it.

The Psalms remind us over and over of God's unfailing love:

> Some wandered in desert wastelands, finding no way to a city where they could settle. They were hungry and thirsty, and their lives ebbed away. Then they cried out to the Lord in their trouble, and he delivered them from their distress. He led them by a straight way to a city where they could settle. Let them give thanks to the Lord for his unfailing love and his wonderful deeds for men, for he satisfies the thirsty and fills the hungry with good things.
>
> PSALM 107:4–9

I clung to God in a way I never knew I could cling to him! I poured my heart out to him every day. I cried a million tears, and I know he caught each and every one. I sometimes didn't even have words for my feelings, but I would close my eyes and at least try to listen for his voice. I was completely open and honest with him—I talked to him like I would talk to my best friend. Like the psalmist, I complained, too, and I was clear about my disappointments. I confided in him about all of my fears. I pouted and wept when I felt alone and lost. I thanked him for being unfailing and for never leaving me in the midst of all that I was going through. I also thanked him when little miracles happened along the way, just as I still thank him, every day, for the priceless gift of my daughter.

I have no idea where you are on your journey. I have no idea whether you have a relationship with God. I'm not here to preach, and I certainly don't think I have all the answers. I'm just sharing some of the solutions that carried me through the most devastating time of my life and brought me to a place of contentment from which I can effectively parent my daughter in a successful co-parenting relationship with my ex. And for me, a huge part of that was realizing that God, who had promised to never leave me, in fact never did. He was walking beside me all the way, and still is.

You are not alone because you have friends

Besides relying on God, I also enlisted a few of my friends to walk with me through the divorce. In my case, these were girlfriends I'd had for years. I told them that, although I knew I needed them, I was too much of a basket case to know how they could really help me, except to love me and listen and help me sort out the details of my life. They did—and it was an incredible help.

Others are in different circumstances. Maybe you moved recently and don't have close friends close by; maybe your marriage has been in trouble for years and you've been concentrating on that to the exclusion of developing or maintaining friendships. In that case, you may want to look among your church family, your own extended family, or your divorce recovery group (all the more reason to find one, if you haven't yet). Think for a moment: Who in your circle of influence right now could be a companion in the process?

I needed to know that I had at least three people I could call at 2:00 a.m.—or who would just get in the car and come over if I asked. I needed to know that I could be completely real with them, that I didn't have to worry about what they thought of me—whether they agreed with me, or whether they had any good ideas. I just needed to know they were there (and that it was okay to cry off all my makeup with them, too!). One of the three friends I chose had been through a divorce and co-parenting her kids for about eight years already, so I could count on her for experience, perspective, and understanding.

Who are those three go-to friends in your life? Who can you enlist to be a sounding board for your divorce recovery and your co-parenting journey? Feel like you're past the worst of the crisis? Pick your three go-to friends anyway—because life throws us some surprises along the way. You may think you can handle it all alone, but tomorrow something may happen that completely throws you for a loop, and you'll need those friends. Besides, one of the best things you can do for your kids is have a plan to handle your own emotions and frustrations. Your kids aren't your counselor, they're not your confidants—they're your kids. If you have a healthy plan in place before crisis hits, then you'll already know what to do when it comes, and you won't turn to your kids in desperation.

Identify three people who may be able and willing to serve you in this way. Even if they don't live near you, even if they live in another state, they're only a phone call away. Write down their names below. In the next week, do yourself (and your kids) a favor and contact each of these three friends. Don't be shy or vague. Ask if you can make them your top go-to friends and count on them if you need to call at 2:00 a.m. Write down the date you call each.

_____ Called: _____

_____ Called: _____

_____ Called: _____

As always, I challenge you to not skip over these blank lines! Do the work.

Having a hard time coming up with three names because of your circumstances? Then make a different list. Identify the ways you'll find three people who can serve you in this way. Maybe talking to your pastor would help, or finding and getting involved in a divorce recovery group, or attending an adult Sunday school class at your church.

You needn't walk this difficult and lonely journey alone.

Home Alone Anyway

I'm sure that many of you, as soon as you saw the title of this chapter, "You Are Not Alone," responded mentally, *Oh, yes I am! I'm absolutely alone way too much of the time!*

I hear you. I remember watching my daughter wave goodbye as she rode away for a ten-day visit with her father – leaving me home alone during our first Christmas apart. I had known the day was coming, and I knew it would not be easy. Even though I was happy for Angelia because she was going to her grandparents' house and would have a wonderful time with her dad's family, that inner ache still arose when I waved goodbye. Sometimes the ache happens on a school night when she goes home with her dad after a school open house. Sometimes it happens before a long weekend away. As a mom who deeply loves her daughter, it's natural for me to feel sad when she's away; but there's a huge difference between missing my daughter and being lost without her. There's a huge difference between functioning with stability even while I miss her, and collapsing into such grief and dysfunction while she's gone that all I can do when she calls is to weep into the phone, making sure she knows what grief she's causing me by loving her other parent.

> *I never wanted to be my dad's only reason to live ... That's a lot of pressure to put on a kid!*
> TINA, AGE 27

As I waved goodbye that first Christmas, I knew that I had a choice: I could walk back into the house crying and then feel lonely and depressed for the next ten days – or I could smile and decide to choose joy for myself. Thankfully, I had anticipated and planned for the moment, so I asked God to remind me of his truth that I am never truly alone, that he is with me and will never forsake me – and then I opted for fun!

One of the reasons I was able to act in joy is because I had already made an intentional decision: I was *not* going to let Angelia be my only reason for living. She's my greatest gift and my greatest blessing on earth, and parenting her is one of my very highest priorities. But I owe it to her, as part of providing the stable and healthy life I want for her, to never make her responsible for my happiness. I chose to create other places of joy and fun in my life so that when she was away at Christmas, or even on a long weekend, I could keep functioning and stay steady. I'm not saying I never shed tears from missing her; I'm not saying that I don't still, even now, feel that inner ache when I wave goodbye. But I've worked hard to find enjoyable ways to stay busy and involved when Angelia is away, and that has been a great benefit to her.

Living alone can be a shock to the system. No matter how much arguing or fighting happened in your past marriage, that other adult in the house was someone to come home to in the evenings. Living alone can bring a new level of silence and quiet that can be terrifying. It came as a surprise to me to discover that quiet can also be beautiful and enjoyable.

Are you an extrovert, like me? Are you an introvert? One of the biggest light-bulb moments of my life came when I fully understood what it meant to be an extrovert. That moment came in college when I took the Myers-Briggs personality test, which measures different aspects of how personalities function. I was one of the most extreme extroverts my professor had ever tested. He explained what that meant: Being an extrovert, I gain energy being around people. Leave extroverts alone for long periods of time, and they feel depleted of energy—exhausted. The reverse is true of introverts: Introverts gain energy from being alone; being around other people gradually drains them of energy. Neither of these tendencies is good or bad; but knowing yourself empowers you to get what you need.

Introverts are not necessarily shy. Many introverted people are national celebrities and seem to be the life of the party when they're in public. Being introverted doesn't mean you can't be social and enjoy large crowds of people. Introversion is just a personality type that implies a need for frequent solitude to recharge one's batteries. The opposite is true of extroverts; their need is for frequent socializing.

The Myers-Briggs personality test is a tool that can help you as it has helped me. If you've never taken it, or if you have but don't remember the results, please see the Myers and Briggs Foundation website at www.MyersBriggs.org. I encourage you to take the test—or find another personality testing system—so that you can understand better how you are wired. That will allow you to intentionally plan your life in a way that's most rewarding and enjoyable for yourself—which will ultimately be good for your children.

You might also learn something about the differences in personality between you and your co-parent—and how your temperaments work best together. Just remember that no personality is morally superior to any other—only different. Understanding your unique differences will help you communicate more effectively.

I write all this partly to explain why, when I became a single mom, I already knew that I don't enjoy being left alone for long periods of time. Aware of this personality trait, I had to be intentional about how I spent my time when Angelia was away with her dad. To be honest, I've sometimes wished that I were more of an introvert, because then I would have enjoyed the quietness at home. Whether you're an introvert or an extrovert, it's important that you create a workable and enjoyable plan for the times you'll be home alone.

Handling the Handoff

Does it sound like I'm underlining the need for preparation? I am. We can't let these potentially lonely times surprise us, and we can't just wing it when they get here—not if we expect to handle them well. And the first step in that preparation is to think about the handoff itself—the actual transition time when your children are leaving. If you're facing your first long time apart from your kids, or any time you expect the time alone to be especially hard, ask a friend to hang out with you that day—to be there when you do the handoff, and then go with you afterward to do whatever the two of you enjoy. Knowing yourself—being able to anticipate what you can or cannot handle—is important. I've often made plans for the day that Angelia is leaving to meet a friend at a local restaurant and then go see a new comedy movie that night. Who wouldn't want an extra reason for Mexican food and then movie popcorn and chocolate?

Your choice of activities might be different. You might plan to meet a buddy for a game of basketball at the Y, or enlist a couple of friends to come over and work on that project at home you haven't gotten to yet, or go fishing. Whatever your idea of fun with your friends might be, make it happen. Don't let pride get in the way. Enlist friends to be part of the process so that you can make the handoff and the time without your kids that follows whole and healthy—for you, and for your kids too.

Once you've decided how to handle the handoff and what will happen in the few hours that follow, I encourage you to create a plan for how you'll spend the rest of your time enjoyably. Here are some suggestions:

Get Your Mind and Heart in the Right Place

You'll be better able to spend your time wisely and enjoyably if you're conscious of where you stand in relation to God and others. Here are some activities that, besides using some of those "empty hours" in an enjoyable and constructive way, help guide your heart to see your situation clearly. God is still in charge.

Focus on God's faithfulness. Make a list of the things you have to be thankful for. Write down each person you love and ten reasons why. Rather than sitting alone feeling sorry for yourself, write letters to people you care about. Make a list of five people to write to while your children are away, and by the time they are due to return home again, have each of those names checked off your list. Today emails and text messages are more common, but why not send a real letter occasionally, in your own handwriting? What a surprise blessing that will be to those five people.

Write a thank you letter to God for the gift of your children and the daily blessings of a home, heat, and food on the table. Regardless of your financial status – and any of us who've been through a divorce have, at one time or another, been barely getting by – if you have a warm place to put your head at night and your children have been going to bed with full tummies, then you have many reasons to celebrate. Life might not be as you'd always dreamed it would be. And you might hate being alone, especially if you're still seething with anger at your former spouse. Give yourself a mental vacation from the negative thoughts. Choose instead to focus on the good things in your life. If you have a job that pays you each month, if you have a car that runs (even if barely), step back and be grateful. Don't let all that you don't have right now overshadow what you do have. Many times on my single-parent journey I've had to squeeze every ounce of good out of every dollar; but through it all I've been so grateful for a warm home, a hot shower in the morning, and a box of mac and cheese in the pantry. Write down a list of all that you *do* have. In time, things will be going even better.

Keep things in perspective. I've said it before and I'll say it again: Every year, life will get better, and every year, you'll find yourself better able to cope with it. Every awkward and frustrating challenge co-parenting hands you will be an opportunity to learn – and you will grow. It won't always hurt the way it hurts today. You won't always be as frustrated as you are today. I know, because I have been on this journey for years myself. It doesn't ache today the same way it ached the first time I waved goodbye to Angelia. I am stronger now, and more stable.

You're already stronger than you think. With every word, as you keep reading, you're getting stronger still. You're growing and getting healthier every day. Tears may still come now and then, but the day will come when you look back and think, "Wow! I can't believe it's been two years already (or ten years). I'm so glad I never gave up! Not on my kids, and not on *myself.*"

You'll have some lonely days while your kids are with their

other parent. When those times come, take a minute to remember the truths I've just spoken. This time will be over soon, and your children will be back home. Be sure they have a calm, determined, well-grounded parent to come home to.

Ask your friends to hold you accountable. Remember those three go-to friends we just discussed? Ask them to check in on you when you're home alone. When they do, be honest with them—admit when you're struggling.

Why is that important? When people are troubled, when they're struggling, then they're vulnerable. One of Satan's most effective schemes is to seduce people into addictive behaviors that seem to numb or make them forget the pain in their lives. Many divorced parents turn to alcohol—at bars or in the privacy of their homes—to numb the pain. Others have returned to a drug habit. Many people get led to destructive websites that offer an initial sizzle, but end up destroying the heart and the soul. Pornography, for example, is available at a click of the mouse, as are gambling websites. Even the strongest Christian needs to commit himself, ahead of time, to not be led astray during the weekends he's home alone.

Talk about your temptations with your friends. Ask them to hold you accountable. Encourage them to ask you, at any time, how you're doing in resisting these addictive temptations. If you've struggled with addictions before, of any kind, encourage your friends to create boundaries and safeguards to protect you. Use software programs like *Safe Eyes* to govern Internet use. For the sake of your children, do whatever it takes to put hedges around your heart so that you can be the most whole and healthy person in their life.

Have Fun!

It's doubly true in the single parenting world that all work and no play makes Jack a dull boy. Even worse than dull—unhealthy. Here are some suggestions for building opportunities for fun into your life.

Have a party. Invite others (other single parents, single friends, couples from work, a neighbor you have been meaning to connect with) to come and share an evening in your home. It doesn't have to be anything more than an eclectic potluck meal served on disposable paper plates. Have everyone bring a game to play and a food item to share. Many others who would have otherwise been alone for the evening will appreciate having something fun to do.

I have done this at Easter, Thanksgiving, and Christmas. It's wonderful to have a house full of laughter and fun (and it's a great way to not have to cook a big meal for myself). I have invited people I barely know and others that I know well. One gal who came to my Easter get-together a few years ago said, "When you invited me for Easter, it really gave me something to look forward to. I usually spend the holiday alone, watching TV, and feeling depressed; but this year I've had something to look forward to all month!" My effort to avoid my own sadness and create fun for myself turned out to be a blessing to others who would have otherwise been wandering through the day alone.

Sometimes you just have to make your own fun!

A party like this doesn't have to cost anyone much money. All I do is open my home, buy disposable plates, cups, and utensils, and put on some music. Everyone brings one item to share, and suddenly you have a ten-course meal and a bunch of wonderful people to fill the table.

One year, Angelia called while I was having a Thanksgiving gathering. She heard all the music and noise and asked what was going on. When I told her I was having a Thanksgiving party, she actually seemed a little bummed that she was missing out on the fun. Isn't it much better for her to have a mental image of mom laughing and having fun with friends, than of mom sitting on the couch alone, crying—and have to wonder whether I was okay? I was definitely okay—more than okay. Instead of surviving the holidays, I thrive on the holidays, whether Angelia is here or not.

Have a movie-and-popcorn night. If you don't feel up to entertaining a large group, ask a friend to join you for dinner and a movie. If you're up to it, why not go see a doubleheader (two movies back to back), with dinner thrown in there somewhere? If you want a quieter evening, rent a couple of movies and stay home for delivery pizza and microwave popcorn. For me, a two-hour movie can be a great source of therapy (especially a gut-busting comedy). And it's certainly cheaper than $120 for an hour with a counselor!

Give your life away to others more lonely than you. An orphanage, a nursing home, or a homeless shelter would appreciate your time. Find out what they need and get involved. Volunteer to serve a meal to the parents of children in the intensive-care unit at your local hospital. Make the decision to share your smile, your hands, and your love to lighten someone else's load. No matter how difficult life is, someone else is worse off, and would love to be in our shoes, divorce and all. The parents in the ICU who are hoping for even one more day of life for their child would trade places with you in a heartbeat, if by doing so they get their child back, whole and healthy. It's all in how we look at it, and how we look at ourselves. We are blessed beyond imagination to get to love and parent our children, even if we do so as co-parents after divorce. Our glass is more than just half full, it's overflowing!

Enjoy the solitude. Introverts, this is where you shine. Pick up that book you've been looking forward to that's been collecting dust on your nightstand for lack of time. Listen to a favorite music CD by candlelight. Take a walk at a local park. Enjoy the fun of pampering yourself. Take a long bath. Sleep in every day. Or, if you're one of the more practical and energetic ones, clean out a closet or a junk drawer that's been driving you nuts for the last year.

Pick one of your "good intentions" and do it. What have you been meaning to get to all year? Commit to getting just one of those things done before the kids return. Build that bookshelf, fix that car in the garage, repaint that old table your aunt gave you ten years ago, make that scrapbook of photos—challenge yourself to accomplish one major goal while the kids are gone. I'll warn you: this one's addictive. You'll feel so much better having finished that task that you'll look forward to the next time the kids are away so you can cross off the next item on your list.

My favorite idea: travel somewhere new. Save fifty bucks a month for a year, and talk one of your friends into doing the same. Then pick a fun destination both of you are excited by, and go explore someplace new during your kids' summer or Christmas or Thanksgiving visit with their other parent. Or better yet, take a cruise! You may be able to get a great rate in the off-season.

Maybe none of those ideas are what really floats your boat. Whatever your personal idea of fun is, I challenge you now to look ahead on your calendar and begin to create a fun plan. Even though it's normal to miss your kids, don't let your "normal" become "lonely" and "depressed." And after you've made your plans, tell your kids about the fun you're going to have. Let them think they're the ones missing out, not you. You're relieving them of an unwelcome and unrealistic expectation to make you happy. And if they really seem to feel left out, you've found another activity to plan for when they're home. Let them in on the fun next time.

CHAPTER 4

Finding Your Stability

The end is the beginning ...
STACY MORRISON, *Falling Apart in One Piece*

In chapter 2, I mentioned how useful my participation in DivorceCare was for me in those difficult days after my divorce. Many helpful things came out of those sessions, but one of the most powerful and most helpful for me was a quote that seemed to jump off the screen in a DivorceCare video: One of the presenters said, "After my divorce I realized I had to get on with my stability."

I had expected the line to be something like, "I had to get on with my life." But what he said was so much more powerful: "I had to get on with my stability."

You, too, need to get on with your stability. Your kids need you to get on with your stability. They need to see you laugh and smile, and they need you to tickle them and snuggle with them. They need to know that you are okay and that you are strong.

The first time I sat down with Sarah, she had been recently separated, having learned that her husband had been unfaithful for years. He'd given her the classic line: "I never really loved you." Brokenhearted, she couldn't speak more than a few minutes without beginning to sob. She had three small children at home. After having been a stay-at-home mom for their whole marriage, she was completely at a loss on how to survive the divorce and the pain that she was feeling.

I saw Sarah again about a month ago, now three years past her divorce. I almost didn't recognize her. She is stronger and more confident than ever! She moves with confidence and strength. Her expression is joyful and sparkling.

Sarah is the living example of Mavis Hetherington's research on the post-divorce timeline we discussed in chapter 2 — broken and shattered in the beginning, and more alive than ever a few years later. As we chatted, it was clear that her life is moving forward. She's going to college, happily raising her children, and they are all very active in church. She's thinking about dating again, but not rushing into it. I wish I could show you a video clip of the "before" and "after" of Sarah's journey. What a transformation! I celebrated with her and encouraged her to keep moving forward and to continue seeking God in every area of her life.

Though no one can go back and make a brand new start, anyone can start now and make a brand new ending.

CARL BARD

If Sarah can get on with her stability, so can you.

Here are some suggestions that might help.

Consider Counseling

Counseling might scare you to death. In fact, some of you might want to punch me for even suggesting it. (Good thing you can't reach me, huh?) But before you get upset, consider this: Talking to a counselor can be the number-one key to unlocking healing in your life. It can be a crucial tool that speeds up the process of getting to your stability. Counselors are, in a sense, like doctors. (Many of them *are* doctors.) They spend years researching, studying, and investing their own money and resources to find a cure for a particular kind of pain. They devote their careers to the idea that they can truly help people process their emotional baggage and find a healthier, more whole, and functional way to live. And most of them truly care about you and about your life.

I encourage you to find a counselor and give it a try. If you're uneasy about it, commit to just three or four visits. After that, decide whether to continue. There are different types of counselors, and different ways to find them.

Most churches have a good list of local counselors. You can probably just call your church office and ask for a few referrals.

The school counselor at your children's school – who is well aware that your children's well-being and your own are closely connected – will be able to recommend local counselors.

You can go on-line. Do a Google search for "counseling resources in _____" (your city). You'll be surprised how many resources will pop up.

Counseling can be expensive, and your budget may be tight; but some places offer counseling on a sliding scale, and you don't need to be embarrassed to ask. Even if counseling stretches your budget beyond where you think it will stretch, your kids will benefit for their entire lifetime if you can get to the healthiest and most stable version of you. What price tag can you ever put on that?

Consider taking your kids to a counselor as well. Many programs, including DivorceCare, have classes designed just for children. Whether in formal counseling or in a class such as those offered by DivorceCare, your kids will need an opportunity to process their pain with an objective party who can be an extra voice of wisdom and encouragement for them. When I felt that Angelia would benefit from counseling, I put my pride aside and asked for the sliding scale so that I could afford to take her. I did the same thing when I asked for help for myself.

If you find the right counselor, you'll have found someone who will listen, who will give advice, who will let you fall apart completely in your sessions – but more than anything, you will find affirmation for what you are doing right. And I'm confident that you are doing much that is right – after all, you're still reading this book, and that means you're searching for answers and direction for yourself and your co-parent and your children. I applaud that – in fact, I give you a standing ovation for caring enough about your kids to find resources, to get ideas from others. I applaud you for caring enough about yourself to grow. I applaud you for the hard work you're already doing. Keep moving, keep learning, keep growing, keep healing. Recovery doesn't happen overnight; but for those who work at it, as you are doing, it happens.

Your Child Is Not Your Confidant

Many of you would agree with me that the weight of divorce is a heaviness beyond imagining. The burdens of finances, complicated schedules, and starting all over in just about everything, all at once, can be more than one person can bear. In these times of distress and vulnerability, let me gently remind you of one of the most common mistakes people make when going through a divorce: pouring their emotions and hurts out on their kids – using their children as a combined counselor and confidant and sounding board for all of their pain. This may be especially common when the kids are teenagers, because they seem old enough to understand what you're going through.

Please don't do this to them. They have their own pain, and it's hard enough on them to carry that. Your pain needs to stay in your backpack, not theirs. You're all going to hurt, you're all going to need help, and you're all in this together; but you're not in it as equals. Your children need you to be stronger than they are.

Listen to the unspoken voices of your children asking you, "Please be strong and stable so that I can know everything will be all right. Talk to someone else about your pain and anger. I don't understand all of these changes in my family – but I need to know that you're okay. I depend on you. If you're lost, then so am I." In my work with children of divorce, I hear the almost continuous refrain that they need their parents to be stronger than they are. In times of crisis and turmoil, in times of uncertainty, they want Mom and Dad to have it all together. You might have to fake a smile for a little while. You might have to take it hour by hour, day by day. But it's critical to get past being hurt and stuck and keep moving forward – for your kids.

Consider what happened to Joey when he was twelve: "When my mom was sad and falling apart, I was the one she came to and told all the horrible details. I remember her crying and distraught, usually already having had too much to drink, telling me about the rejection from the men in her life. I felt desperate and scared – not just when she was telling me this but all the time. I was being put in the role of an adult counselor for my mother – and I was still in middle school.

"I would listen to my mom crying about having been rejected by various men, with her strongest anger reserved for my dad, and about how she didn't know if she could pay the rent or the light bill. I often cooked my own meals and always did my own laundry. It was like someone took any sense of internal stability I had and just shredded it. I was worried about money and about where we would live. I remember crying myself to sleep and feeling alone in the world because my mom's world was a wreck and it was up to me – at twelve years old – to figure out how to fix it. I felt like I had to make her happy, had to make sure she didn't drink too much. I was her dad and her counselor, all in one."

This type of role-reversal between parent and child is what psychologists call *parentification*.[2] A child's personal needs are sacrificed in order to make the child responsible for taking care of the needs of the parent. Because they love their parents, children are often accommodating in this: they give up their own need for comfort, attention, and guidance in order to address the needs and care of the parent. In parentification, the parents abdicate their responsibility and transfer that responsibility to one or more of their children. Hence the child becomes *parentified*. That child is the "parental child."[3]

In the article, "Harming Your Child by Making Him Your Parent," Dr. Samuel Lopez De Vectoria explains there are two kinds of parentification: emotional and instrumental. *Emotional parentification* forces the child to meet the emotional needs of one or more parents and usually other siblings too. This kind of parentification is the most destructive. It robs the child of his childhood and sets him up for a series of dysfunctions that will incapacitate him in life. As the result of having been made the parent's confidant, these children have difficulties having normal adult relationships when they reach adulthood.

Instrumental parentification is when a child is made responsible for the physical needs of the family. This child may take care of the children, cook, and so on, relieving the parent of these responsibilities. There's a big difference between this and having the child learn responsibility through assigned chores and tasks. The difference is that, in instrumental parentification, the parent robs the child of his childhood by forcing him to be an adult caregiver with little or no opportunity to just be a kid. The child turns into a surrogate parent, responsible for his siblings and parent.

Parentified children can become very angry in life. They will tend to have a love-hate relationship with their parent. Grown to adulthood, this child may not know where his anger at others, especially friends, boyfriend/girlfriend, spouse, and children, comes from. Their anger may be explosive or passive. It often erupts when another adult places expectations on them that might trigger their parental wounds of emotional exploitation. The parentified adult child may find it difficult to connect with friends, spouse, and children.[4]

What Joey's mom should have done was enlist the help of an adult friend – a counselor, a pastor, a coworker, a neighbor, a sister, or a brother – anyone willing and capable of filling that role. It was not Joey's job to make sure his mom was happy or that she would be okay. It was her job to get out ahead of her own pain and to help Joey process the pain he was feeling.

Let Joey's experience be your wake-up call. Learn from it. Don't lean on your children for emotional support. Don't make them your counselor or confidant.

Pay Attention to Parental Adjustment

Research has shown that one of the key reasons children of divorce may suffer is something called "parental adjustment." Researchers Amato and Keith explained it this way:

The psychological adjustment of parents is a significant factor in children's well-being. There have been many studies examining the relationship between divorced parents' psychological well-being and children's well-being. Of the 15 studies that have examined this relationship 13 found that there was a positive relationship between the mental health of parents and children's mental health. That is, children whose parents are better adjusted fare better than children whose parents are not adjusting well.[5]

It makes perfect sense. Children, as they grow, always have one eye on their closest parent for clues as to how to move through life. If that closest parent — you — is a basket case, where's the example your children need for a well-adjusted, balanced, and healthy life? So as you begin to adjust emotionally, financially, and physically in those first tough months after divorce, remind yourself *daily* that you need to find healthy new patterns in this new chapter of your life — for your children's sake, because their well-being is inextricably tied to yours. You can become the parent, like Sarah, who adjusts well to the transition and who is strong and stable for your children. You can keep yourself clearly focused on moving forward and getting on with your stability.

The University of Montana's research on constructive interventions for divorced parents includes a strong affirmation about the power of one great parent: "The main ingredient for children's emotional adjustment appears to be the support of a competent, caring adult who is able to offer warmth and responsiveness as a buffer against the adverse effects of divorce."[6]

This book is filled with clues and ideas on how to aid your post-divorce parental adjustment and keep it on track; but the best advice is to keep your mind focused on solutions rather than on problems. Be a part of the solution, rather than creating more problems — for your kids or anyone else in the co-parenting equation. Stay positive. Regardless of the past, regardless of who hurt who the most, regardless of the present challenges you face — make up your mind to be the competent and caring parent who stays engaged with the heart of your children. In full knowledge that your children's welfare is directly tied to how stable you are, be their anchor through the storm.

Know What You're Committed to, and Stay Committed

Make a commitment to yourself right now that, regardless of how hard things might be for you right now, you're going to put your big girl/big boy britches on and make the very most of the time you have with your kids – this week. Adherents to AA just try to live one day at a time; let's follow their example and commit to doing things right just for right now. Don't worry about your entire life.

Whether you have the kids for two days, two hours, or all week, do something out of the ordinary with them. Let them be kids! Give yourself permission to laugh and enjoy the time. Go to the park and throw the Frisbee around. Go to the lake and feed the ducks. Go to Sonic and get a milkshake; take a walk in the park while you drink it. Let your kids see you laugh.

Even if you feel like you're completely faking it, dig deep to muster up some joy for a couple of hours. Be the joy in their day. Be the hug they come home to, or the smile they need when you pick them up from daycare. Don't spend your few precious hours with them each night complaining about work, or talking about your finances, or bad mouthing their other parent – be the person you want them to become one day. Model it. Walk it. Strong words and good intentions have to be backed up; strength must be walked. And you do have the strength to keep walking.

Choose to be whole. Believe that you are in the process of healing so that you can see above and beyond your circumstances right now, and stay committed to where you are going. Know that you will be stronger with every new day. Remember you are not alone; enlist a true set of friends to walk through this journey with you. If you choose to be stable for your kids, you will grow in wisdom and strength as you grow into that stability. If I can do it – if I can survive my own sadness without leaning on my daughter – and I have – then I know you can do it too.

*AWAKEN!**

BY TAMMY DAUGHTRY

I see YOU reflected in beams of light,

When HOPE awakens after night.

Come show Your GLORY through each ray,

Bring LIFE to the heart that's gone astray.

AWAKEN inside the will to LIVE…

To not shrink back, my HEART I give –

To Your purpose, to Your will,

Not understanding, I TRUST You still.

Hope RESTORED, we live on.

The night's been dark and yet it's DAWN.

Through the struggle our lives are shaken,

And yet I shout,

"Oh, soul … AWAKEN!"

---

*(written at sunrise as I asked God for continued healing …)

PART TWO

It's Not About You— It's About The Kids

CHAPTER 5

Kids in a
Post-Divorce World

Now, who will pay for pizza?
WILLIAM COLEMAN, age 4

It was just a few days after Steve's second marriage, their first full day back from their honeymoon, and he was feeling relieved and happy. The ceremony had gone well, and participating in it with him and his bride had been all five of their kids — two from his first marriage, three from hers.

But he hadn't even eaten lunch yet that day when his peace was shattered by a note handed to him by his daughter, Jerri, who turned and fled as soon as she'd pushed the note into his hand. He watched her go, puzzled, then uncrumpled the note and read: "How can you stand in front of the preacher and make those promises to somebody new when you stood in front of a preacher once and made the same promises to my mother, and you didn't keep them?"

**Statistics —
do they define
you or will you
defy them?**

Jerri isn't the only child of divorce who has asked that same question. She's just one of the few who has actually verbalized it.

The life of a child of divorce is not the same as the life of a child from an intact family. A child from an intact family would never have to ask Jerri's question. Whole books, many of them, have been written about the needs of the children of divorce, not just when they're minors but also when they've grown to adulthood and still carry the marks of the difficulties they encountered after their parents' divorce. The statistics are scary.

What will define the life of your children? Will it be your

divorce? Or will you and your former spouse defy the negative statistics and create a new story? What will your cooperative co-parenting promote in your kids?

I'm convinced that with intentional effort and consistency, children of divorce can have as much opportunity to thrive as any child in any household. Great parenting never comes easy; great co-parenting is even harder. But hard doesn't mean impossible.

Researchers have said that six predictable outcomes exist for children after divorce.[7] I say that all six can be overcome, and that you and tens of thousands of other co-parents just like you can be the beginning of a new and healthy pattern of expectations for children of divorce. I know many amazing young adults, and you probably do too, who are living stable and healthy lives even though they came from divorced families. It can be done – and it starts with you.

Let's take a look at those six predictable outcomes. And while we do, I'll show you how you can defy the negativity and create good outcomes for your kids.

Parental Loss

The simple fact that you are reading this book defies parental loss. You're still in this game, still committed to your kids. Is your co-parent still in it with you? Maybe, maybe not. That's something over which you have no control, although you can try to influence it.

Having one committed and loving parent in the game, even after divorce, can actually be more effective and beneficial than the parenting pattern experienced by many kids living in traditional, intact families, who may see their parent every night but have no emotional connection or deep relationship. Some children in intact families feel abandoned. It's not that their parents don't live under the same roof with them – it's that their parents are too involved with work or friends or social activities. Having two parents in a house does not equal emotional stability for a child. It all depends on how those parents relate to their child.

Still, having said that, two good parents are better than one good parent; and if you don't have a co-parent in the game with you, here are a few suggestions that may help your children:

- Enlist a mentor. You can't be all things to your children, so find a man or woman who will support your children and help fill in the gaps. Programs like the Big Brother/Big Sister organization can be a help.

- Enlist a surrogate grandparent. Ask an older person in your church or community to be part of your family's life, helping to plug the hole left by an absent parent.

- Enroll your children in a program that fosters community with other kids and leaders, such as Boy Scouts or Girl Scouts.

- Talk to one or two of your kids' aunts or uncles in your immediate family. Tell them your concerns; ask them to step in and help. One young man I know of, Anthony, at the age of thirteen stepped into the role of being a male mentor to his nephew after the nephew's father walked out of his life. I don't know whether someone asked Anthony or he simply saw the need and moved to fill it, but eighteen years later Anthony is still that young man's father figure. Anthony recently drove fourteen hours each way to enroll his nephew in college. He talks to his nephew every week to see how he's doing in college, what books he needs for class, who he's dating and what they're up to—and he challenges his nephew and holds him accountable. Anthony, at the age of thirty-three, has been a father to the fatherless for eighteen years.

Solutions can be found. We owe it to our kids to be resourceful and find them. We can't be too prideful or too embarrassed. For the sake of our kids, we must look the obstacles straight in the eye and find a solution.

Economic Loss

Economic loss may be hard to avoid. Nearly all of us who've gone through a divorce have struggled with this. The period after my divorce was the most difficult time for me, financially, of my adult life; but money doesn't define value. Even if your kids have less tangible "stuff" after your divorce, and you go out to eat less and rent movies more often than you go to the movies, they have more important things. Even though your kids may — undoubtedly will — complain about having less disposable income, they know at some level that they need your time and your listening ears and your smiling face more than they need the next Xbox game or Play Station. And you definitely know it.

Divorce will, most likely, knock you on your tail for a season, financially speaking. But who decides if you stay knocked down? You do. Are you going to wail and complain, or are you going to stand up, dust yourself off, and move forward?

The best part of the struggle for me was that I learned how little we could get by on. I remember, when I was first single again, going to Target and buying just two bowls, two glasses, two mugs, and two sets of silverware. I didn't need more than that — there were just two of us, myself and my little fourteen-month-old, Angelia. She was still using sippy cups then, and we had her little Elmo bowl and plate, so with just two of everything else, we had an extra set! I rented a small, simple, two-bedroom duplex and lived humbly for several years. I was working from home at the time, so one bedroom was my office and the other we shared. We painted one wall pink, and Angelia called it the "happy house" because it was our little fun place to live. When we first moved in, Angelia was in her crib. Two years later she was on a daybed, and all I had room for was a little mattress I would pull out at night to sleep on. Humble? Yes. Maybe a little embarrassing sometimes? Sure. But nothing can replace the sweet, deep joy that we shared, mother and daughter,

> It's not money but you that make your children rich!
>
> EVERTON ANTHONY

and the priceless memories we made in our little duplex. I will always remember it with great fondness.

I couldn't afford any extras at the time, so I focused on what was most important. Food, shelter, clothing, and love. Some of the sweetest and most valuable times we spent together during those two years were spent playing outside in the backyard, going for walks around the neighborhood (with me pushing Angelia in the stroller, pointing out trees and flowers on the way), cuddling up and watching Barney (she'll kill me for telling about that now), and playing in the bathtub until she turned into a little pink raisin. None of these things were expensive. None of her clothes were new. I never went for a pedicure, and I probably went a year or more between professional haircuts—but we were happy! I truly believe we were *rich* compared to some of the families whose homes may have looked nicer on the outside but were hollow inside.

No matter your circumstances—if you have to get a second job and eat the generic brand of cereal for a year—it's okay. The richness is in the loving relationship you have with your children. When they see you smile, when you hold them and tickle until they giggle—that is all they will need. If that means you have to toughen up and face these challenges and be resourceful in finding solutions so that your little financial ship doesn't founder, then so be it. That's what you have to do to protect your children's giggling time.

Sometimes brainstorming with a friend can help you find ways to tackle your financial hardships. Be willing to ask for the help you need, and do whatever it takes to keep moving. Don't let financial hardship define your children's lives in these all-important years.

Lack of Parental Competence

The third indicator of negative outcomes for children after divorce is called *lack of parental competence.*

I'll confess: I laugh when I read that because, if we're going to be honest, incompetent parents can be found everywhere—in married families, in rich families, in poor families.

What makes a great parent? Is it the size of their mansion or the price tag on the car they drive? Is it the country club they belong to or the course they golf on? Is it the nail salon they get their manicure at or the social club they play tennis with? No, it's their commitment to love and protect their children and to raise them up in a healthy and stable environment. The great parent is the one who has clear and consistent boundaries and does not let life dictate his or her success, but rather proactively pursues success and models success for the children. It's the parent who takes time to help the children with their math homework and listen to the details of their day. It's the parent who looks the children in the eye every day and says, "I love you!" It's the parent who lovingly tells the children "no" when it's appropriate, and doesn't try to be a friend to the kids but truly a parent. It's the parent who reads books or attends seminars to gain understanding and to excel in his or her role in the family. It's the parent who humbly apologizes when he or she has blown it, and asks the children for forgiveness. It's the parent who puts the needs of the children over his or her own longing to date and spend time with friends. It's the parent who sacrifices personal convenience in favor of the children's well-being. The great parent is the one who makes a long sequence of decisions in the same direction: toward the best interest of his or her children.

All of those decisions about parenting can be made by married parents or single, rich parents or poor, parents who are successful at their careers or those who are just hanging on. Are you competent as a parent? The fact that you're still reading this book tells me that you're already working hard on behalf of your children. You are already amazing! You are learning and growing, and for that your children will be abundantly blessed.

Forces will be arrayed against you as you continue to work as a parent after divorce—forces that may diminish your effectiveness as a parent. I'm talking about things like your own discouragement and sorrow and grief over the loss of your marriage and the partner with whom you may have been exploring life for years.

Emotional struggles can distract you from your primary task as a parent. Be aware of that—and determine that your children will continue to get as much of you as a parent as they had before.

More Life Stress

Divorce often means that children move to a new living situation, change schools, change child caregivers, and so on. These changes have lots of implications for the kids. They'll have to make new friends, they may not be able to see extended family as much as they're used to, and they'll have to create a new life routine between two homes. Even under the best co-parenting arrangement, these changes are stressful for kids. And while you cannot eliminate the stress that comes with having parents divorce, you can mitigate and counteract the stress of these changes. Here are some suggestions:

- Keep the kids in the same school if possible, even if you have to move to accomplish that.

- Make every effort to allow them to continue in their extracurricular activities: band, dance, swimming, scouting, sports, and so on.

- Help them find someone to talk to: a guidance counselor at school, a children's counselor, another trusted adult with whom your children are comfortable, a youth pastor, or coach. Kids always need an outlet other than parents, and kids who find a caring adult to fill that role are blessed. Those relationships often extend well into adulthood. Provide opportunities for your child to connect with someone they can air their pain and frustrations with. You can't force a relationship, but you can let your child know you'll be glad for them to find another trusted adult and to arrange ways for the relationship to grow.

- Don't over-schedule your life. Allow time and space to relax and enjoy your children, to take walks around the park and be together. Even though you may find it's easier for you to keep busy to keep your mind off the divorce, it's best to follow that pattern when the kids are at the other parent's house. When they're with you, try to slow down. Take time to bake cookies, plant flowers, walk the dog together, go hiking, and just relax.

- If you do have to move, help the kids keep in touch with friends, either by arranging visits or weekly chats on Skype.

- Let your kids grieve. They feel it, and they need to say it. Listen to them with love.

- Keep as many "familiar" things in their environment—bedspreads, toys, etc.—as you can.

- Remind them that you are a family, no matter what walls you live within.

Parental Adjustment

Parental adjustment is all about you, about how well you adjust to the monumental changes that have taken place in your life. Does all of that change you? Does it make you self-absorbed? Throw you into a depression? Send you out on the hunt for a mate? Are you in danger of becoming someone your kids don't recognize?

I'm not here to sugarcoat things for you, or to say that being divorced is easy. I don't have the one-size-fits-all answer on how to process your pain. I do know what helped me. I intentionally got involved in a few groups like DivorceCare and went to a women's weekly Bible study. I sought out healthy people to befriend me, and I wasn't too proud to let others know when I was hurting. I was careful to avoid filling up the holes in my heart with "stuff," or to turn to alcohol or substances to escape my reality; I just faced it, as much as that hurt. In the long run, it hurt less because I didn't create new problems for myself. I cried my way through the pain many nights, but I kept moving forward. I had three "go-to friends," and they heard from me often. I kept my eye on where we were going, not where we were at. I kept believing that one day it would all be better—and it is.

As I said earlier in the book, it is not always going to hurt the way it hurts today. Your pain is not going to engulf your future. Give yourself time, find a counselor, go to the DivorceCare classes, enlist appropriate adults to help you process your pain—just don't let the pain paralyze you or define your future. You have a destiny to walk into—but to get there, you have to keep marching up this mountain, giving your children a path worth following. Don't settle. Don't give up. Rest when you need to, but keep waking up and doing the right thing each day. Eventually, you'll look around and see just how far you've come. Then it will be your turn to help encourage another wounded walker.

Inter-Parental Conflict

By the time a couple gets to the point of divorce, their children have probably been seeing their parents fight for years. After the divorce, the fight just continues—and most often, it happens through the children. If you want to approach co-parenting responsibly and lovingly—and you do, or else you wouldn't still be reading this book—you're going to defy that statistic. You are going to be different. You are not going to wound your children by continually yelling and arguing over money and visitation times. You're going to be radically different from the norm and defy this negative impact on your children.

The next generation (your grandkids) depends on you to rise above the norm when it comes to inter-parental conflict. Don't let your past determine your future. In your relationship with your co-parent, be willing to say and do the right thing. Be willing to leave the harmful things unsaid and to sacrifice your own desires. In other words, be willing to do whatever it takes to raise your children well.

> Your children's life will be a story told ... how will that story read, And what will the story say about you?
>
> TAMMY DAUGHTRY

I believe that, twenty years from now, the researchers will

be saying something totally different from what they're saying now. They'll be saying that the children of divorced parents who were raised by cooperative co-parents who met once a month at TEAMM meetings and worked together for the children's good have proved to be as well-adjusted and emotionally and mentally stable as any child. The books will point out that those parents who were able to protect their children from inter-parental conflict and who adopted healthy co-parenting skills have proven that children can still thrive after a divorce.

That won't happen if we simply resign ourselves to what the observers of society have noted. It will happen only if we determine to make a difference – not for ourselves, but for our kids – and point our families and our society in a new direction.

The old books said one thing. Let the new books say another!

CHAPTER 6

Parenting Forward

No Do-Over...

Baby toys to car keys
Etch-A-Sketch to checking accounts
Saturday morning cartoons to Wall Street updates
Tuesday night homework to college applications
Today ... is almost tomorrow
No rewind buttons
No deletes
As time passes ... no do-over!

TAMMY DAUGHTRY

Having grown up in Denver, I'm an avid Broncos fan and will forever cheer for John Elway, the all-time number-one quarter-back. Growing up, I never missed a game. My mom and I watched on our little black-and-white TV, and my dad's family cheered in the loudest and craziest ways. Denver was a great place for a football fan to grow up because Broncos fans are hard core. I've seen just about everything painted in orange and blue, the Broncos' colors: houses, cars, even four-foot piles of snow. Orange snow — who knew?

I love the complexity of football. I love the intensity of training to win. I love the fact that it takes eleven people on the field to be an effective team. Football is not a one-man (or one-woman) sport — everyone has to work together to accomplish the goal. Things happen quickly; every move matters. If any player, offense or defense, is even one second off during a play — even a half second — everyone is impacted. Victory does not come easy, and it does not come for one player acting alone (not even for John Elway). Behind the scenes, even at the junior-high or high-school level, the training is intense and grueling—definitely not for the light hearted. Football is fast. Football is furious. Football is fabulous!

A few years ago, I realized that co-parenting is a lot like football. It takes a team to raise children after divorce—and not just any haphazard, thrown-together team. Co-parenting well—and do you really want anything less for those kids you love?—is like moving the football down the field.

Think about it: First, the offensive team huddles up and confirms the plan. The players move into formation. The ball snaps and is in the quarterback's hands. He looks down the field, and has about two-and-a-half or three seconds to pick a receiver and release the ball—and he doesn't throw the ball to where the receiver is, but to where he is going! It's a predetermined plan, precise and specific. No guessing; no winging it. The exact rotation of the ball, the power behind the throw, even the arc of that leather ball's flight—all are determined by where the receiver is going, and by the type of defense the quarterback is facing. Everything has been pre-determined by the quarterback and receiver, working with the offensive coordinator who's now on the sidelines. They're all on the same team, and they have a common goal—to win the game. Whatever it takes, no matter the cost, they are in it to win it.

All of that is true, too, in only slightly different ways, for you and your co-parenting team. First, you have to be on the same team; and right now many of you, I'm sure, don't feel that way. For some, the pain of divorce is still too fresh—the sense of betrayal by someone you loved and trusted, guilt for the role you played in bringing your own marriage to an end, the confusion and hurt of watching a set of friends and a set of in-laws and family that you expected to be intact forever disintegrate into factions. You probably feel that some of your team members are playing for the opposing side. But to move the ball, you'll have to find ways to work together for a common goal. That's not easy. It's not for the weak of heart or the easily discouraged. If you are going to play the game of life and raise your children well, you must be on the same team with your former spouse and you must work together to move your children down the field toward the goal: a successful and joyful adulthood.

What a concept: creating a team with the person you couldn't

Tips from the Child's Perspective*

Tips for Parents—If your children could ask you out loud to put some safe boundaries in place, they might sound something like this:

1. **Don't put us in the middle.** We are not your messenger. We are not your confidant. Please don't make us choose sides. It's just not fair. We want to love you both.

2. **Be available.** You may be ready to talk about the divorce. We may not be there yet, at least, not with you. In the meantime, let us know that we are free to ask any question without a bitter or defensive response. As we heal, we may feel a need to fill in the holes in our history. If we can talk about it (not fight about it or justify it), we can learn from it.

3. **Reflect.** Think about why your marriage failed and be ready to tell us what you have learned—when we ask. We want desperately to know that we aren't destined to divorce as well. Tell us why you are proud of us. Be specific. Make a list of the good things that came from the marriage (including us!). Write down the reasons why you first fell in love with our other parent. If we have the positive characteristics that once drew you to your ex, tell us.

4. **Understand that our healing process is different than yours.** Our pain began as you started recovering. As kids we can only cope with the difficult choices you have to make. It's often not until we're adults that we have the emotional maturity to begin healing. Be patient.

5. **Adjust for our convenience.** It's hard for us to balance the time we

*From *Generation Ex: Adult Children of Divorce and the Healing of Our Pain* by Jen Abbas (Colorado Springs: Waterbrook, 2004). Used by permission.

do life work with! But that's the situation you're in, like it or not. You brought children into the world together, and now, in order to work in the best interests of those children and to keep from causing them any more pain than they've already experienced, you

spend with both sets of parents, especially around holidays and special events, and especially if we feel we're in a no-win situation. When parents have different sets of rules and expectations, it makes it hard for us to know what to do. We need as much stability and consistency as possible.

6. **Be prepared for a wide range of emotions.** Certain events may trigger a response. We may have blocked out a lot of memories as a way of coping. As adults, those memories may come back without warning, and we may respond to them with anger, confusion, or any other emotion. Sometimes, in frustration, it may seem directed at you. Realize that our response is a delayed reaction to something that you may have already processed.

7. **Tell us good things about _____, our other parent.** We have a right to love you both. Talk to a friend or counselor or pastor about the things that drive you crazy about our other parent. Don't tell us. We need to know the good stuff.

8. **Legitimize our loss.** Please don't force us to feel okay with what happened. Most likely, we will always feel a loss because the divorce is just as significant as losing a limb or sense. It doesn't mean we can't be healthy, but life will always be just a little different for us than it is for others.

9. **Tell us you love us.** We can never, ever hear it enough. Sometimes it feels like the divorce of your ex was really a divorce of us. We saw from your example that love is conditional, earned, and fleeting. Prove us wrong by loving us completely and consistently.

need to find a new kind of relationship with your co-parent. The task before you, just like the task that faces the Denver Broncos on any given Sunday afternoon, requires precision and determination in every move. It requires the ability to look above the chaos and see the end zone—to look above the "noise" and interference of life and keep your eye on where your children are going. Not on where they are now, or on where you are now—but on where they need to be in five years, ten years, fifteen years: moving into adulthood.

My Baby, the Grown-Up

Those children of yours are someday going to be grown-ups, out on their own.

How is it that we wake up and our little babies have turned into adults? When did snuggling up to a good bedtime book turn into trying to catch them between text messages and Internet surfing? When did tossing the football with someone who could barely hold it with both hands turn into setting up his dorm room in college? Once we couldn't see the light at the end of the tunnel—now we just wish we could slow down the train. Time is passing at the speed of life, and we will never have this exact minute again.

Parenting of any kind, including co-parenting, doesn't come with rewind and do-over buttons. We have one shot. As in football, if you fail to move the ball during the second quarter, you don't get to go back and do the second quarter over. It's gone. What we do today will affect the entire life of our children. We can't afford to waste even a minute.

The words you speak today—for good or ill, spoken unwisely in pain and anger about your ex or spoken in love and wisdom to the children-growing-toward-adulthood—will find roots and grow forever inside your children. When you handle your children's hearts carefully, you sow life into their soul, life that will remain there and become a resource to them in the future. And when you fight with your co-parent in front of your children, you sow doubt and pain that hurt and hobble them in the future. Your selfishness and anger about the past furnishes your children's future. Is that really the legacy you want to leave them?

Listen to what Joey remembers of childhood: "I wish I could erase so many memories: The angry phone calls and the tug of war over my time, the endless negative comments about my dad from my mom, the stress over just buying school clothes. I always hated the beginning of each month because that was when, at my mom's request, I would have to call my dad and ask why the child support was late. I hated the last week before school because my dad would take me shopping, and my mom would be jealous and mad about the two hundred dollars' worth of school clothes I came home with. The emotional outbursts of each parent have traumatized my life; it's been years, and I can hear those voices still. Have I forgiven and moved on? Yes – but can I ever truly forget or undo the pain? No. Do I wish I had an erase button for painful memories? Yes! Do I often wish I could trade my childhood for someone else's with less pain and agony? Yes!"

Many divorced or single parents lose sight of the *right now* that is in front of them because they are so focused on the pain of the past. Yes, we must heal from the past; but we cannot lose sight of the exact moment right now, the moment our children are living in, and the impact this exact moment is having on our children.

For those of you who are in the middle of a separation, deeply hurting, I beg you to sit up and pay attention. I remember the darkest days of my life; I remember not knowing how I was going to take even one more step in the journey. I remember the shattering of my dreams and the broken pieces of my heart. Even so, I want your full attention right now. Set aside for the moment thoughts of who is to blame for your divorce; forget, just for now, what the other parent did wrong, forget who did or said something unfair. Set aside your own feelings of guilt or regret. Let's focus on your children and their future.

I'm not here to give glib answers or cliché responses. I know life hurts – I've been there, and I'm still there today. But on behalf of your children, I tell you: it's time to wake up and realize you don't

A New Family Bill of Rights

I came across this "New Family Bill of Rights" in *Mom's House, Dad's House: Making Two Homes for Your Child*[8] and wanted to share it with you. Please fill in the blanks with the names of your children. No empty spaces!

• _____ has the right to have two homes where he or she is cherished and given the opportunity to develop normally.

• _____ has the right to a meaningful, nurturing relationship with each parent.

• Each parent and _____ has the right to call themselves a family regardless of how the children's time is divided.

• Each parent has the responsibility and right to contribute to the raising of _____.

• _____ has the right to have competent parents and to be free from hearing, observing, or being part of their parents' arguments or problems with one another.

• Each parent has the right to his or her own private life and territory and to raise _____ without unreasonable interference from the other parent.

get a do-over — no do-over for today, no do-over for this morning, no do-over for tomorrow. You cannot erase their pain and you cannot undo their memories. What has happened in the lives of you and your children in the past, whoever was to blame for it, is done and can't be undone. If that's a source of some regret for you, stop allowing yourself to stagnate in that regret, stop beating yourself up, stop beating up your former spouse — and start parenting forward.

What do I mean by *parenting forward?* I mean moving the ball down the field, toward the goal. I mean realizing that the broken play you just completed, on which you lost yardage, is already in the past and you'll gain nothing by dwelling on it. I mean, in this awesome task of parenting the children God has entrusted to you, you live as if you believe Philippians 3:13 and 14: "But one thing I do: Forgetting what is behind and straining toward what is ahead, I press on toward the goal to win the prize for which God has called me heavenward in Christ Jesus."

Every day your children are in your home you will find at least ten opportunities to speak meaningfully to them. Will you speak words of life? Or will you speak words that diminish the life growing within your kids? I can't tell you the number of unexpected conversations I have had with Angelia in which I've had to decide how to respond. She asks questions about her life, about her dad, about our past marriage. And when I respond to her, I have a choice: I can allow myself the self-indulgence to respond in a way that makes me and my home look better than her dad's, or I can exercise self-control and respond positively and helpfully into her life.

Most divorced parents are hurt and angry. There are deep resentments that can fester and that are, in many cases, completely "justified." However, when angry and resentful parents react out of the hurt inside themselves, it just creates more hurt and pain for the children. A very common conversation could go something like, "You know, your mom is the one to blame for this divorce. If it wasn't for her filing, we would still be married." Or something like, "I told your dad I was willing to work on the marriage, but he decided he wanted to leave. He never gave us a chance. We could have gone to counseling or we could have gotten help; but no, he walked out and he never looked back." These kinds of conversations are common, but you must rise above common if you want to keep your child's heart whole.

At first, when the hurts are raw, you may find this difficult; but I have found that co-parenting exercises an emotional "muscle" inside that gets stronger with use. A combination of self-control and a peculiar internal clarity keeps me focused on Angelia's life and where she is going, rather than on me. As that "muscle" gets stronger over time, you'll find it easier to measure your words carefully, to filter out the knee-jerk responses of anger, condemnation, betrayal, and instead choose words that are uplifting and more about your children's future than about your past.

Here's what Tina says about it: "I wish my parents had realized that all the destructive chaos they dragged me through hurt me to my very core. Their negative words may have been about each other, but it was my self-esteem that was damaged. The stress my mother made me feel about money and child support has had an impact on me all my life in the area of finances. They put me in the middle of so many decisions and conversations that were their job—not mine! I know that their intent wasn't to destroy me—what they really wanted was to destroy each other. But the harsh truth is that in their ignorance and through their destructive words and their fury with each other they created a deep hole in my soul that I may never be able to repair."

Your children do not have to repeat the experiences of Joey or Tina—or me. They don't have to be wounded by the unknown. The fact that you are reading these words and opening yourself up to find a better way is a big step in the right direction. I'm confident that you will do a much better job at co-parenting than Tina's parents did, even if you have to work hard for every bit of cooperation from your ex. Simply because you're willing to do your part, you have the chance to parent your kids radically different and radically well, even after divorce. If you incorporate even one idea out of this book, your children will benefit all their lives from that one choice. If you choose to incorporate two ideas, their benefits will double. No one has more influence on a child's life than a parent, and you, all by yourself, can be the difference between life and death to your child's soul.

Here's the bottom line: You have one shot in this co-parenting journey. What will you do with it *today* so your kids won't spend the rest of their lives wishing for a do-over or an undo button?

CHAPTER 7

Your Children
Love You Both —
and That's a Good Thing

Just because someone wasn't a very good spouse
doesn't mean they can't be a great, much-loved parent.
MARTHA AUSTIN-WHITE

Love is patient, love is kind....
It is not rude, it is not self-seeking.
1 CORINTHIANS 13:4, 5

Having grown up between two houses, two cities, and two co-parents, I can tell you from personal experience that children love *both* parents. Your children have that right; and no parent who loves them should deprive them of that right. You and the children's other parent might drive each other crazy and you might have years of unresolved conflict or hurts between you, but your kids love you both. Children of divorce wish they could stand up to their parents and say, "Stop talking bad about my dad (or mom)! Don't make me choose who I love the most. I don't want to know the bad things that you did to each other. I just want to love you both!"

> One Heart, Two Homes. If only parents would place this concept above their own angst and anger ...

Particularly in the cases of separation or divorce, co-parents often have such strong ongoing negative emotions about their former spouse that it can cloud every conversation with the children. Many parents bring up the past to try to prove to their children that the other parent is irresponsible and not trustworthy; but all that does is hurt the children. Telling your children how good you are and how bad the other parent is can irreparably harm your relationship with your children; they may end up resenting you instead of the other parent.

Keeping your children away from their other parent is equally as damaging (unless there are issues of safety, which we'll discuss in chapter 17). Loss of important relationships is a critical issue for children, and children from divorced families are particularly at risk for this. Children accustomed to seeing both parents every day before separation often see one of them only four days per month after separation and divorce.[9]

Many co-parents' negativity about the other parent stems from jealousy. Tina shared with me her honest thoughts about the financial imbalance between her parents and how it hurts her: "My least favorite time is the few weeks before school starts. My dad always takes me shopping for school clothes, and it drives my mom nuts. He has more money than she does, so he tries to help me out; but that makes Mom jealous, and I have to listen to her rant when I get home. She brings up mistakes he made when I was a baby and retells the stories of all the times he disappointed her. I just want her to smile and be happy for me about the school clothes. Instead, it always has to be about her."

Here's the irony: Parents who act like Tina's mom are trying to make their kids think badly about their other parent—but it usually backfires. First, it makes the kids feel bad about themselves. Why? Because kids identify with *both* parents, as I'll discuss under "The *I* Factor," below. And also because of another concept called the *divided self.* The unified family the kids thought they belonged to has now been divided, and when you rage about all the negative details about the other parent, the gaping hole between the two halves of your child's heart becomes a huge cavern.

Imagine a heart-shaped piece of paper with your child's name on it. Imagine yourself taking that paper heart in both hands and ripping it in half, then taking a pen and poking holes in the two halves of that heart. Figuratively, that's what you're doing to your child's heart when you bad-mouth his or her other parent. The paper has no feelings—but your child does.

Talking harshly about the other parent also makes children despise the one talking. A mom or dad who tries to play the martyr or the victim in the eyes of their children will see their children lose respect for them. Children will try to distance themselves from the one who is being so negative.

Some of you have already done some of this—spoken ill of your co-parent to the kids in an attempt to create some solidarity in their relationship with you against your ex. Perhaps you've enlisted your kids into your army in the battle against your ex and tried to justify that behavior in your own mind by telling yourself that you're just speaking the truth. But whose truth is it? Certainly not your ex's. Whether we like it or not, every divorce has two sides, two stories. But a divorce that involves children has more than that, doesn't it? It also has the truth that your children will figure out for themselves. Resist the temptation to try to make them see only your truth. You'll inflict lifelong wounds on their heart.

Trust me, if the other parent is truly irresponsible, if the other parent has serious character flaws, the kids will see that on their own. You don't need to point it out, adding painful drama to an already painful situation—your kids will see it firsthand. Wouldn't you rather be the safe place for them to talk and be understood than the war leader they can't stand to be around?

Research has borne all of this out: "Mothers may function as gatekeepers to father involvement after divorce (Pleck, 1997) and maternal hostility at the beginning of divorce predicts less visitation and fewer overnights 3 years later" (Maccoby & Mnookin, 1992).[10] It's clear from this that maternal anger and dissatisfaction impacts kids. In plain language, don't let your unresolved anger keep your children from seeing their other parent. Your kids need both of you. That is how God designed them. Don't alienate or eliminate their father from their lives if he is willing to be involved and is a loving, safe father. And don't try to turn your kids away from their mother to make yourself feel superior.

Let me resort to more research to bring home my point – this time taken from college students whose parents had been divorced at least ten years: "Feelings of loss reported by college students a decade after divorce (Favricius & Hall, 2000) indicated that they wanted to spend more time with their fathers in the years after divorce. They reported that their mothers were opposed to increasing their time with fathers. When asked which of nine living arrangements would have been best for them, 70% chose 'equal time' with each parent, and an additional 30% said a 'substantial' number of overnights with their fathers."[11]

Ouch! That is hard to hear for some of us. I hate to sound like I'm picking on moms, but statistically moms are much more likely to come out of a divorce with custody of the children, and the custodial parent gets more say in the children's schedules. If you keep the kids from their father, you're probably doing it (at least subconsciously) to hurt him. But the ones you are hurting the most are the kids.

The research project I cited just above also pointed out that: "Students experienced a painful longing for the absent parent that might have been alleviated with more generous visiting arrangements."[12] Take a moment to let that soak in. Your children have a *painful longing* for the absent parent. You can't fill both parental roles in your children's lives, no matter how badly you want to believe that you can; and when you make decisions out of anger or jealousy or plain old selfishness, it's the hearts of your children that are wounded.

And when your children are allowed to spend time with their other parent, what is the result? "Children with involved, loving fathers are significantly more likely to do well in school, have higher self-esteem, and do well in other ways."[13]

Because you love your kids, encourage them to spend time with their other parent. Please don't be an obstacle to giving them the best. As research shows, the father's role is critical in all areas of your children's life: educational, emotional, social, and developmental.

If you have good reason to believe that your kids are in danger of physical or emotional abuse when they're with the other parent, that changes things; we'll cover that in chapter 17. But in most divorces, when both parents are interested in being involved in every aspect of their kids' lives and the children are not being abused or neglected, then allowing the children to spend as much time as possible with both parents is ideal.

When your children talk to you about the other parent, your responsibility is to handle the information as neutrally as possible. Your kids need to be able to express their own opinions about their life, their successes, their hurts, and their frustrations — being a neutral listener will reap huge rewards over time. Resist the temptation to inject angst and anger into those conversations with your children just because of your own issues arising from your past. It will only be counterproductive.

The I Factor

Kids know they come from both Mom and Dad. And when you say anything about their other parent, they will internalize it — meaning they'll hear it as if you said it about them. Make sure you understand that: Any description you give of the other parent is going to sound to your children as if you are saying it directly about them. So, to love your children, to build your children's self esteem, to minimize their divided self, use only words that are hopeful and life-giving.

Dads, if you tell your kids, "Your mom is a raging lunatic; she's emotionally unstable," then your kids are going to internalize that thought like this: "I'm a lunatic; I'm emotionally unstable."

Moms, if you say, "Your dad is so irresponsible; he never pays the child support on time. He's such a loser." your kids will internalize that as, "I'm irresponsible; I can't be trusted to pay things on time. I must be a loser."

You don't believe it? I promise you, it's true. One high school girl I interviewed recently said, "I want to scream when they start the negative babble. When my parents say mean and cruel things about each other to me, it makes me feel broken, like I'm a shattered piece of glass or a broken mirror and all I see in the reflection are their angry faces staring back at me. I hate it!"

Let's look at the *I Factor* in a more positive light. Moms, you can say, "Your dad is a hard worker. He's creative and a really talented songwriter." Dads, you can say, "Your mom's excellent with money. And she can always be trusted to take care of things on time."

> It doesn't take strength to hold a grudge; it takes strength to let go of one.
> JESSE (ACTOR JOHN STAMOS), FULL HOUSE

I can almost see you throwing this book in the trash, shouting, "No way, Tammy!" I know it's hard—believe me! But remember: life is no longer just about you; it's not about what comes easy. You're a parent now, and if you're in this game to raise emotionally healthy and stable children, then hear me: those kids needs to hear positive words from you about their other parent.

Can't think of anything positive to say? Then it's time for an exercise. I want you to pick three positive characteristics about your children's other parent, things suitable to say to your children, and write them down below. If you're stuck, just try to remember what it was you loved about that person in the first place.

Don't opt out of this! It's important.

Positive Characteristics of Your Co-Parent:

1. _____

2. _____

3. _____

If you left the blanks above empty, don't read on. You're cheating your children out of a healing gift—your gift of life-giving words. Sit here for a minute, find a pen, stop cursing me under your breath, and pick three things you can tell your children that are great characteristics about the other parent.

You have a choice here. You can choose health for your kids, or you can choose to make their lives harder — which will it be? Will you take the easy way and become just another statistic — another angry ex-spouse who does nothing different from most other divorced parents, thereby hurting your own children? Or will you suck it up and try something that seems ridiculous because it's the right thing to do for your kids? I know you love your kids — you wouldn't have made it this far in the book if you didn't radically love your kids. So get off the couch and get in the game.

What were those three characteristics? Remind yourself. Rehearse them. And the very next time you see your kids, say them out loud to your kids. Your kids may look at you as if you've grown a second head, but say it anyway — and say it with a positive, uplifting tone in your voice. If they ask you what you smoked for breakfast, just shrug and say, "I just think you have a great Mom [or Dad]. Sure, we've had our differences. But I also think _____ [say again the three positive characteristics]." I promise you that your children will immediately respond. You won't be able to measure or touch the affect within them — you may not even detect it; but deep inside, your children will feel a sense of hope and freedom that is life-changing!

Say those three things out loud and often. Consider yourself a cheerleader for the other parent. Yes, I did say a cheerleader for the other parent. And no, I'm not smoking anything right now. I say this because as you begin to shift your mindset from anger and hate to neutrality and even positivity about your former spouse, you'll be unlocking a prison door inside of you and letting yourself out. When you continue to do this over and over, you'll actually begin to have a natural response that is positive and life-giving.

Are you doing this because the parent deserves it? Are you doing it because life has treated your fairly? No, you're doing this for your children. The side benefit is peace and freedom inside your own soul! Imagine not being anxious or upset when you see your ex. Imagine not having any tears or rage when your kids leave for a time with your co-parent. Imagine not having to lie in bed and replay the scenes of yesterday over and over and over. If you make a hard and fast decision to build up your former spouse (for your kids' sake), you'll begin to think and feel differently. If, on the other hand, you hang onto hatred and bitterness, if you are consumed by the past, then everyone, including you, loses. If you let go and move on, working toward a healthy mindset for yourself and your children, then you win and your kids win.

A quote that I heard long ago has transformed me: "Hanging onto anger and unforgiveness is like drinking poison and expecting the other person to die." If you hold onto bitterness, letting it consume your every waking moment, you'll end up sick and in a negative cycle that leads to emotional death (for yourself). I have been in that place. I have cried for hours, to the point of almost throwing up, because I was hurting

> I have set before you life and death, blessings and curses. Now choose life, so that you and your children may live ...
>
> DEUTERONOMY 30:19-20

or disappointed by life. But the moment came when it was time to get up off the floor and wipe away the tears and get on with my stability. I believe that time is here for you. Cry as needed, but decide it's time to get moving and that stability is your goal.

As you continue to say the three positive characteristics about your co-parent I want you to also say, out loud, to your kids, "It's okay for you to love us both!" Eight words. Yes, I know they're hard to read and even harder to say; but for the sake of your children and unborn grandchildren, I want you to say them. Right now, say them out loud with me: "It's okay for you to love us both!" One more time: "It's okay for you to love us both!" If you're reading this on an airplane, you may need to turn to the person next to you and explain that you weren't suggesting anything inappropriate but simply rehearsing something important for your kids.

When I discussed this concept with Leslie, she said, "If I'd ever heard those words from either of my parents, even just one time, my entire life would have been different. I'd have grown up with a lot less anxiety and stress. And that would have made room for more joy and more laughter and more happiness!"

If you've been guilty of negative talk about the other parent in the past, don't beat yourself up. If you said something horrid to your kids about their other parent just twenty minutes ago — then right now is the time to make a whole new start. You might even apologize to your kids for the way you've talked about their mom (or their dad), and that you have come to realize that it's okay for them to love both parents. That would be a great time to start talking up those three positive characteristics about the other parent! Hard? Yes. But what you'll be doing for your kids is bringing healing out of hurt.

Get the Picture

I know some of you want to push me off the mountain with these ideas that are so much harder in practice than they sound, but if you truly love your kids, and if you truly want the best life for them, here's one more amazing tool for your tool belt.

When Angelia was little, I wanted to find every way possible to help her know that it was okay with me that she loved her dad, even though we were divorced. I wanted to tell her with my words and my actions that I was thankful (yes, thankful) that he was in her life, and I never wanted her to feel like she couldn't talk about him in my home. So I tried something that seemed simple. She was a toddler at the time, and it seemed appropriate for her age. I printed out three photos of her and her dad, put them in magnetic frames, and I placed them on the refrigerator down at her eye level. I didn't announce it. I just put them up one day. It was fun to watch her discover them! We had other kid magnets on the fridge — letters, numbers, gadgets, etc. — that she loved to play with while I was cooking dinner. On the night that she saw her daddy's photo on the fridge, she was so excited. She said, "Mommy, that's my daddy!"

I said, "Yes, honey, that's your daddy. He loves you very much. I'm so happy you have such a great daddy. You can talk about him anytime you want to." She smiled up at me—and then she leaned in and gave the picture a kiss. My heart rejoiced because I knew we had struck a chord that would resonate for her lifetime—and that she would not have to grow up with all the sadness and darkness I had felt. If I could create a home where it was okay for her to talk about her dad, to miss her dad, to love her dad, then it would be a much stronger foundation for her future than I had known.

Today Angelia is eleven, and we still have photos on the fridge of her and her dad. I have also given her a cork board in her room where she can put photos and memorabilia of her dad and her other family (stepmom, stepsiblings, grandparents, cousins) on display. I encourage you, no matter how old your children are, to do that too, and do it soon. Whether the photos are on the fridge or on a cork board in their room, tell your kids you want them to have a place to put special photos and items from their other parent. If they look at you funny, just say, "I want you to know it's okay to love us both. You don't have to pick a favorite." Depending on their age, it may take them awhile to get used to the idea.

I often hear from our seminar attendees that the photo idea was the one thing they did after the seminar. They printed a photo or took a photo of their kids with their other parent and displayed it in their house immediately. It's a gift you give your kids that has invisible and lifelong rewards.

I would love to hear back from you if you have other ideas that communicate your positive feelings about your co-parent. Go to our website and tell me your idea, and I'll share it with other co-parents. We can all learn from each other. We may be at different places on the timeline and on unique journeys, but we all have one common cause—to love and co-parent our children into whole and healthy adults. Share with the rest of us your ideas for how to do that better.

Handling the Handoff

When I was first separated, just beginning this journey of co-parenting, I decided that Angelia's dad and I wouldn't discuss life details when we were handing her off between my house and his. Research literature gives sound evidence for the importance of this approach: "Transitions between two households is an arena where children may have angry or painful feelings."[14] Why take the chance of making those feelings worse? Especially when I had first-hand experience in how difficult those hand-offs could be — whether or not they took place in a 7–11 parking lot. Remember Leslie's story? Parents screaming at each other, the flashing lights of police cars, the public humiliation, the tears.... I never *ever* wanted to expose Angelia to anything like that, not even a quieter, more private version.

Although her dad and I were, relatively speaking, getting along well and weren't likely to end up in any dramatic fight, Angelia was only two years old — and even a "normal discussion" between her dad and me, recently divorced as we were, might feel awkward or uncertain to her. So we agreed that we would never discuss things at transition time. Nothing big, nothing small — nothing! We decided, instead, to have a co-parenting meeting once a month and talk through the details of Angelia's life (physical development, discipline concerns, upcoming schedule details, picking a pre-school, buying school clothes, etc.). It has worked well.

The best part is that Angelia never gets stressed out when we transition her — we are all smiles and hugs and encouraging words. For Angelia, this is her normal. She has told me how her friends at school hate to have their divorced parents in the same room, how painful it is when they fight; Angelia has never heard us fight, and she never will. Read that again: John and I have been co-parenting for ten years, and our daughter has never heard us fight, and she never will.

I'm no superhero, and neither is John. We just set our minds, from the beginning, on the goal of protecting her heart, and we are committed to that goal. Meeting it requires that we handle every detail with conviction and consistency. Sure, it would have been easier, at times, to say, when her dad was dropping her off or picking her up, "As long as you're here, can we talk about how we're going to pay for these dance lessons? Because ..." But we agreed way back in the beginning how we would handle it, and we have stuck with it, with one or two exceptions in ten years of co-parenting. Angelia benefits from an easy, smooth transition between the two people she loves the most. No stress, no anxiety, no tears, no loud voices, no harsh tones, no anger, no frustration, no drama.

Easy? No. But then, it's not about me, it's about Angelia. Her dad and I were intentional about that decision. We decided what our goal was and how best to meet it, and then we agreed to that course of action.

Making the Most of the Time You Have

In a study of children five years post divorce, the researchers said: "We found that 30 percent of the children had an emotionally nurturing relationship with their father five years after the marital separation, and that this sense of a continuing, close relationship was critical to the good adjustment of both boys and girls. These men had worked hard to earn the parenthood that fathers in intact families customarily take for granted."[15]

You may not have as much time with your children as you wish you had — but even so, you have the opportunity to focus on them and be completely present when you do have time together. You'll have time for the distractions (things like paying bills, reading the newspaper, zoning out to mindless TV shows, reading email, working on your laptop, playing golf, going shopping, and so on) when your kids are with the other parent. When they're with you, be fully engaged. Look them in the eye when they talk to you and listen to what they are saying.

Having an intact, traditional family is no guarantee that parent/

child times will be meaningful. In many traditional families, parents and kids just pass in the hallway, or maybe share a quick greeting. Why? Because the parents work late or are focused on other priorities. Just because everyone lives under the same roof doesn't mean that parents are active and involved. It takes intentionality to be a great parent.

Make the very most of the hours and days and nights with your children. All too soon they will be driving away to college, and you'll wish you had those hours and days back. Don't let yourself miss a minute. Let the laundry sit another day and do something to fully engage with your children.

And remember — they really do love you both and need you both. Be supportive about the relationship they have with their other parent. It's never about tearing down the other co-parent. It's about building up the children!

PART THREE

Creating a Co-Parenting Team

CHAPTER 8

Five Categories
of Co-Parenting

The ultimate measure of a man is not where he stands in moments of comfort and conveniences, but where he stands at times of challenge and controversy.
MARTIN LUTHER KING, JR.

When I was fifteen, I went on a ten-day backpacking trip across the mountains in Colorado – the most exhausting *and* exhilarating experience I'd ever had. Each day we encountered new landscape to conquer. Some days we waded through mossy swamps with water up to our waists, holding our packs above our heads, praying we wouldn't disappear into some hidden ten-foot-deep hole. Some days looked like a straight shot up; we looked up that steep, rocky path that seemed to wind on forever and thought, *No way!* I can remember how heavy my blue backpack was, full of all that I had considered necessary for ten days. And I remember how many times I wanted to toss that pack over the cliff to my left, because I didn't know how else I could keep going, barely able to put one foot in front of the other, fighting the sun, the wind, and the insistent voice in my head telling me, *Just quit!*

But what a profound and deep character-building experience that was! To realize, part of the way through that trip, that I had survived so far – that in fact I *would* survive. Ten days in the wilderness without any sign of civilization – and I would make it. What an incredible and life-changing feeling it was to know that I possessed strength *far beyond* what I had expected.

I don't know where you are today in your co-parenting journey. Maybe you've been climbing this mountain, exhausted, for years and you just want to push the pack (or your former spouse) off the mountain and sit down and never move again. Just drop out of the game. Just give up. Or maybe you're three weeks into an unexpected separation – overwhelmed, paralyzed, unsure how you'll take even one little step forward. Wherever you are on this journey, I know the mountain can seem enormous. And here I am, telling you that you're going to have to continue hiking alongside the one person most responsible for your distress – for the rest of your life? Broken hearts and all?

> You can never conquer the mountain, you can only conquer yourself.
>
> JAMES WHITTAKER

Sit for a minute and rest. Take a deep breath. Know that you have resources to call upon to help you on this journey. And once you've progressed far enough along it to reach the conclusion that you *will* make it – that you'll be one of those who shoulders your pack for as long as you need to because you have a great reason for doing so, namely, the children who desperately need you to carry on – you'll experience two things. First, as I did in my Colorado wilderness adventure, you'll experience a wonderful infusion of confidence and wonder at your own strength and resilience. And second, you'll find that it isn't all pain and longsuffering. That, in fact, it gets better over time.

The Five Categories

As in backpacking, we need a map and a compass. If we get lost, the map and the compass can help us find our way out and back to the intended course. The information and insight I can give you through this book can serve as your map and compass on this journey, helping you identify where you are and where the road leads.

In the Binuclear Family Study (BFS), a national study funded by the National Institute of Mental Health and the University of Wisconsin Graduate School to explore how families change after divorce, Dr. Constance Ahrons concluded that five categories of co-parenting relationships exist.[16] Why is that important to you?

Because understanding what category you and your co-parent are currently in, you can better strategize where you are going next, and how to get there. In Dr. Ahrons' book, *The Good Divorce,* she describes these five categories. Each of the descriptions below is condensed from the more complete description in *The Good Divorce:*

1. **Perfect Pals** (high interactors – high communicators). Perfect pals still call themselves good friends, even after divorce. Perfect pals stayed well connected, asking about each other's lives, activities, and feelings. They even asked for advice and helped each other out, as friends would. One couple in the study even continued to own a business together after the divorce. Perfect pals stayed connected with each other's extended families. All perfect pals had joint custody; some even spent many holidays together. A common pattern was that these couples followed this type of relationship early after the divorce, but grew more distant, though still friendly, as time passed.

2. **Cooperative Colleagues** (moderate interactors – high communicators). More of the couples in the study fell into this group than any other. Unlike perfect pals, cooperative colleagues did not consider themselves to be friends. Holidays were split according to a mutual agreement – not spent together. Cooperative colleagues talk often, always about the children or possibly extended family, not about their personal lives or feelings. In some cases, the dads had full custody, with the mother having visitation. Cooperative colleagues seem to have the ability to compartmentalize their relationship: They didn't confuse the issues connected to their marital relationship and those related to their parenting relationship. Their desire to provide the very best for their children trumped their own personal issues. Five years after divorce, 75 percent of these couples remained cooperative colleagues, even though most had remarried by that point.

3. **Angry Associates** (moderate interactors – low communicators). Twenty-five percent of the sample were angry associates. Instead of being able to compartmentalize their anger about the

past, they let it spread into related and even non-related issues. With each other they were generally tense and hostile, or even openly conflictual. Most of the custody arrangements were for sole custody. Even five years after divorce most couples were dissatisfied with how things were going. By that time, one-third had transitioned into cooperative colleagues, one-third to fiery foes, and one-third remained angry associates.

4. **Fiery Foes** (low interactors — low communicators). Twenty-five percent of the sample were fiery foes — ex-spouses who rarely interacted. When they did talk, they usually ended up fighting. Their divorces tended to be highly litigious, and their legal battles often continued for many years after the divorce. They were not able to work out arrangements for the children without arguing, and many relied on third parties (lawyer, friend, or child) to settle their disagreements over each issue as it arose. Fiery foes were unable to remember the good times in their marriage; instead, they clung to the wrongs done to each other and even exaggerated them in order to keep building their case. Many of these ex-spouses exchanged their children at the door without saying a word.

5. **Dissolved Duos** (non-interactors — non-communicators). The study had no dissolved duos, since participants were required to be involved in their children's lives. In this category, ex-spouses are usually completely disconnected. The noncustodial parent is usually uninvolved and out of the picture, perhaps out of the geographical area. This creates true single-parent families; the other parent exists only in memories and fantasies.

Which category do you find yourself in? Which do you *wish* you were in?

Let's make a record of it.

In which category would you place you and your former spouse today? Please date it and write it down here:

_____ Date: _____

In which category do you think your co-parent would place the two of you today?

_____Date: _____

Which category do you think is best for your kids?

_____

If the category you identified as best for your kids is not the one you think best describes the current place you and your co-parent occupy, how much effort are you willing to expend to move your "best parenting practices" with your ex to the level you identified in the final question above?

Experts agree that Cooperative Colleagues is the most healthy co-parenting style for children – and also for ex-spouses. Some might have thought, at first read, that Perfect Pals seems ideal; but a Perfect Pals relationship between exes is confusing to the children – and, frankly, it's also emotionally confusing to the ex-spouses. If you and your former spouse have divorced, then your emotional needs should be met elsewhere, and your family traditions should be adjusted to your new lives. This is one of the hardest parts of starting new family legacies. We'll come back to this subject in another chapter, but for now, just remember that your children will be confused after divorce if everything else seems "the same" but you live in two different houses. It might be easier for the parents at first, but not for the kids. Your kids will be hoping, openly or secretly, for everyone to get back together under *one* roof again, and if Mom and Dad seem to still love each other just as much as they used to, well ... why not? And imagine the confusion for everyone when one of the two of you begins to date someone new. Are you going to bring your ex-spouse along on the date, too? I doubt it.

The key to successfully developing a Cooperative Colleagues relationship is for both co-parents to "compartmentalize" the relationship – to understand your reasons for working cooperatively. It isn't so that the two of you can help meet each other's emotional needs. It isn't to give the two of you a chance to share the intimate personal details of your new lives. Your reason for cooperating is to co-parent your children forward into the most healthy and well-adjusted adults possible. To do so, you'll need to discuss schedules and financial matters. You'll need to have searching and thoughtful discussions of discipline and boundaries for each stage of life your children pass through, from potty training ideas to when they get their first cell phone or set of car keys. Co-parenting is real life, lived out in two homes by two caring co-parents who are committed to playing the game on the same TEAMM. The end adult matters most.

Three Models of Co-Parenting

Dr. Mavis Hetherington developed another way to identify the categories of co-parenting: conflicted, cooperative, or parallel.[17] The following is an excerpt from Dr. Hetherington's book, *For Better or For Worse: Divorce Reconsidered.*

> **Conflicted co-parenting** is when former spouses make nasty comments about each other, seek to undermine each other's relationship with the child, and fight openly in front of the child. Aside from being damaging, constant put-downs of the other parent may backfire, producing resentment and a spirited defense of the criticized parent by the child. One ten-year-old said, "When she goes into her usual routine about what a loser my dad is, I just hate her. I can't stand it. Last night I yelled at her to stop and threw my dinner plate on the floor and locked myself in my room. She tried to make up but started with, 'But you know your dad's really irresponsible.' I cried all night."
>
> **Cooperative co-parenting** arrangements are where parents put the well-being of their children first and it is often difficult to attain. These parents talk over the children's problems, coordinate household rules and child-rearing practices, and

adapt their schedules to fit their children's needs. Two decades later, the couples who cooperated were glad they did.

Parallel co-parenting is a mixed blessing. It is the most common form of co-parenting (according to Dr. Hetherington) and is the easiest to implement. These parents simply ignore each other. They do not interfere with each other's parenting or make any coordinated parenting strategies. They usually send communication through their children. The lack of parenting communication opens the door to problems and as children get older monitoring can be difficult. Children can also manipulate or play one parent against the other since they are the messenger.

I hope that these two categorizations of co-parenting models helps you identify where *you* are in the system – and where you might want to grow toward. What would it take to get from where you are to where you want to be? What action steps can you take to improve your co-parenting relationship (for those who are conflicted) or to establish more appropriate boundaries (for those who are perfect pals)?

I hereby give you permission to actually be civil and cordial to your co-parent, and not to assume an ulterior motive lurks beneath everything your ex does or says. Only you know the true motive inside your own heart for how you behave towards your children's other parent, just as only your co-parent knows the true motive inside of his or hers. Every tabloid, every issue of *People* magazine, is full of stories of angry associates, fiery foes, and conflicted co-parents. Sizzle sells! Some of the country's top celebrities have had very public on-going wars over their children, and they have dragged their divorce issues into the spotlight time and time again.

Such publicity has resulted in a sad but widely held misperception: That the "norm" is to hate the other person after you divorce, that you are supposed to fight over the children and make it as hard on the other parent as humanly possible. Each of you was probably encouraged (or are being encouraged now) to "get everything you can" out of the divorce (houses, cars, furniture). I challenge you to be bigger than that — because it's the *kids* who will lose in that equation.

The media often fans the flame of hate and bitterness after divorce, encouraging people to never let their anger go. How often do you see a TV show about divorced parents who actually get along? Are there any "good news" shows that focus on all that is right and working in the world? On behalf of your children, I say: Be the bigger parent. Be nice to each other, in public and in private. Don't make the ballet recitals and the ball games

> If you get up one more time than you fall, you will make it through.
>
> CHINESE PROVERB

about you — they are about the kids. Don't show up with an angry face and put the kids in the middle of a cold war by not speaking to each other. Even if you do truly hate the other parent, even if you have reason to — be the one who chooses wisely, the one who does not drag your kids into the mess. I'm not saying to "stuff it." I'm not saying to ignore your feelings. I am saying that your kids don't need to be the ones to pay the penalty for all that has hurt you in the past. Work out your stuff in private and with appropriate friends or counselors.

Think of it this way: As a co-parent, you have signed up for a lifetime membership in the "Smile Anyway Club!" Even if you're angry inside, show up with a smile, and let your kids enjoy having the two people they love the most in the same room but without drama. Be the leader in the co-parenting team — shoot for cooperative colleagues, and don't settle for anything less from yourself.

Never lose sight of why you are climbing. You're climbing so that every generation that follows your trail will find hope and strength and peace and joy. Pioneer this path; prepare a way for your children to come safely behind. You aren't doing this just for your kids; you're doing this for your future grandkids too.

CHAPTER 9

Take the Initiative: How to Begin Forming a Cooperative Colleague Partnership

How do you eat an elephant?
One bite at a time ...

I recently overheard my daughter Angelia telling her friend: "You're lucky to only have two parents. I have *four* parents now, since my mom and dad are both remarried. Sometimes they all get together for a parenting meeting. I don't know what they talk about, but I sure hope they decide to let me get a cell phone soon!" I laughed; but it reminded me of one of the real benefits of being in a good co-parenting relationship: you don't always have to be the only bad guy.

Angelia has always known that the big decisions are always made by her father and me working together, and that she can't play one of us against the other. After her father remarried, the decisions were made by the three parents, and all three attended the meetings. Now that I am also remarried, there are four parents in the mix. Legally, the decisions are up to her father and me, but since both of Angelia's families are affected by our decisions, we try to make them with all four of us working together.

Humility and a positive tone of voice go much further than pride and frustration!

Recruiting the Team

You may be thinking, *Right ... I've got about as much chance of recruiting my ex, who already doesn't return my phone calls, to join me on this co-parenting team as I do of waking up tomorrow to find half the NFL teams in a bidding war to make me the next Peyton Manning.* It may go better than you expect. After all, the odds are pretty good that, regardless of how things stand between the two of you, you both love your children. And this is clearly all about the kids.

Here are a few suggestions:

Preparation: Before you make the call

First, **psyche yourself up.** Think it through. Prepare yourself to be brave and calm at the same time. Decide how you're going to control your tone of voice. The last thing you want to do in broaching a subject like this is sound like a know-it-all who's trying to tell the other parent how to run his life.

Rehearse. You might even ask one of your close friends to listen as you pretend to talk to your co-parent. Have them give you feedback on your tone and the words you choose.

The call

Make a nonthreatening start. Being careful to choose the time of day at which your co-parent is likely to be at his or her most receptive, call and let him or her know, in a positive tone of voice, that you are going to email some material you've come across on raising children after divorce and would love to get feedback. You might start with something like, "First, I want to thank you for being a loving parent to _____ (use your children's names). I want you to know I appreciate the way you take care of them. In fact, I would really like to get your input on some things because your opinion is important to me ..."

Provide a mini-model of cooperative co-parenting: Ask for input on something small and easy – "What do you think about

Johnny joining Cub Scouts and going to a troop meeting once a week? We would each have to take him on our weeks." "Jenny's been talking about joining the swim team; what do you think?" Don't put your co-parent on the spot by asking for a decision immediately; ask him or her to think it over and get back to you with input because you value their opinion.

Why call first? The tone of the discussion can be established on the phone or on a voicemail; you don't want them to think they are about to be reamed out when they see an email from you. Emails are unpredictable—the actual words you use can express very different messages depending on the tone that's implied, even if that tone is mostly in the mind of the recipient. Calling your co-parent first will help lay the groundwork for a positive tone.

The first email

One heart, two homes. Start by sharing the crucial concept that children need and want both Mom and Dad and that this will give them the best childhood and future life possible. Stress to the other parent that you value his or her role in your children's lives and that you recognize how important he or she is to the children. Tell your co-parent you want to do everything you can to assure the children have a full and rich relationship with both of you, and that the two of you can both put the children first.

Introduce the concept of co-parenting. Mention that you've been reading a book about co-parenting and finding some helpful ideas that you want to share. Explain that the book is focused on parenting the kids, not on your marital past or unresolved issues between the two of you.

Introduce the material. Tell your co-parent that, since you know how much he or she loves the kids, you wondered if you could send, by return email, one or two pages of information that have helped you understand what the kids are going through.

Leave a smile. This is a good time to start the habit, if you haven't already, of always ending your communications with your co-parent in a way that leaves him or her more willing to connect with you the next time. A good way to do that is to always end by expressing gratitude to the other parent for the positive contributions he or she makes in your children's lives.

The second email

Attach the material. Assuming that you receive a positive response to your first email, follow with a second email that includes, as attachments, the two sections of this book – both of which are available as free downloads from our website (www. CoparentingInternational.com). These sections introduce the core principles of co-parenting.

> Page 1: "Categories of Co-parenting"
>
> Page 2: "The Top 10 Things Your Kids Wish
> They Could Tell You"

Can we meet? Ask your co-parent if he or she would be willing to meet for coffee and to talk about those two pieces of paper. Keep it simple and non-threatening. Don't make it sound like you're asking for reconciliation or an opportunity to renegotiate the divorce agreement – make it clear this is just about the kids. Suggest a few possible times over the next month and ask if one of them works.

Make nice again. Be sure to express gratitude for your ex's willingness to read the material and for parenting the kids. Even if you aren't yet grateful, say you are – and sow it with faith that it will soon come to pass. It's amazing how far basic gratitude and appreciation can go as a bridge-builder. Express affirmation for the efforts you see the other parent putting into being a great parent.

Potential Reactions

Now you have to sit tight and wait for a response. If you haven't heard from the other person within a couple of weeks, it would be appropriate to follow up – not in a scolding way, of course, but rather with an "I know you're busy, but I just wondered if you'd had time yet to review the material I sent ..." approach.

As you read the suggestions above, you may have been thinking, *That's not the best approach to take with my ex. I think she'd respond more positively if I ...* Nobody knows your ex-spouse like you do. You know his or her quirks, emotions, prejudices, and strengths. Customize my suggestions above for your own situation; do what works best for you, given your personality, and what works best for your ex-spouse. Just keep the goal in mind: You want to emerge from this discussion, by phone and/or email, with a decision to meet to talk about the future parenting of your kids.

Be careful not to judge too quickly, though. You may know your ex well enough to think you can predict exactly how he or she will respond; but be open to a surprise. God may have already been preparing your co-parent for this message from you.

That's not to say, of course, that all divorced parents will respond well. Here are some of the forms the reaction of your kids' other parent may take:

Positive: Some co-parents will be appreciative. They may be shocked but glad to discover that you want their feedback and input, and will respond positively. If so, thank God for an ex who responds well.

Suspicious: Some co-parents won't trust your motive; they'll think you're up to something. Maybe in the past you've given reason for suspicion, or maybe your ex is just one of those who assumes the worst no matter what. Don't let such a response throw you off. Keep an upbeat and positive attitude no matter what. It might take months or even years to get the other parent on the same page with you, but don't give up. The suspicious ones may agree to meet anyway, because they *do* love their kids, or they may put you off. For now. Keep occasionally providing reminders and opportunities for cooperation.

Defensive: Many people, especially those slow to accept change, get defensive as a first reaction to new information. Your co-parent may feel that you're trying to be the expert, trying to come off as the one who *really* loves the kids, or trying to control the situation. If that happens, stay calm and don't get defensive yourself. Use active listening, repeating to your co-parent what they just said: "I hear you saying that …" Then restate your motive clearly and calmly: "My motive here is simply to work with you, as a team, to co-parent our children in the most positive way possible. I don't want to fight or argue. I don't want to criticize or judge. I just want to share with you some useful information I've found so that we can learn, together, how to do this co-parenting process. I need your help and your input. Our kids will benefit from it – and they'll relish the freedom to love us both without fear of offending either of us."

Tentative: Your ex may think, *This is too good to be true, but what's the catch?* If so, be patient. He or she will eventually warm up to the idea – especially if you're consistent and reassuring.

No response: If the other parent doesn't respond at all, or gives a terse and meaningless response, don't follow suit by shutting down yourself. Remember, you're not doing this for your own sake, but for your kids'. That means it's worth continuing to pursue. Find opportunities, even if only in an occasional email that you aren't even sure is being read, to mention the benefits for the children of a more cooperative approach to co-parenting, and your desire to get on the same page so that the children can have a better life. But be careful to approach this with a nonjudgmental attitude and choosing your words very carefully so that nothing you say seems to cast blame or guilt.

Preparing for the First Meeting

So let's say you've accomplished your purpose: Your co-parent has read the material you sent and has agreed to meet with you to discuss it. Gut-check time! Right now, you're not sure whether you're glad, terrified, or both. Rather than rush into that meeting unprepared and lacking confidence, take the time to gather your resources and plan your strategy. You'll feel much more confident if you know your goals and know how you're going to attempt to accomplish them.

Know your agenda: As some of you have no doubt already discovered, the hard way, it's frustrating to have a long-awaited discussion only to find out that all of the things you wanted to say have fled your mind. Don't let that happen with this all-important discussion. Study the next chapter's suggestions on what to include in the discussion. Know what is crucial for you to say, and what can wait till next time. If all goes well, you'll have other opportunities. Make up your mind to be satisfied with what you're able to accomplish this time. Whatever else happens, it's a start.

Body Language: Give some thought to what you will be saying through your nonverbals. What can you do to put your co-parent at ease? Smile. Avoid fidgeting. Talk slowly. Unfold your arms. Let your physical attitude communicate that you're relaxed and nonaggressive and open.

Using "I" Messages: Prepare yourself to speak in "I" messages as much as possible to lessen accusations or defensiveness. About the worst thing you could do in a conference like this is to point your finger and say, "You...." The other person will undoubtedly hear "You're doing it wrong." I statements remove perceptions of accusation. Communicate your own feelings and thoughts: "I'm hoping to ..." "I'm concerned about Jenny's grades. I want to find a way to help her get her homework done."

Do a little research: Backing up your statements with tangible information is especially important if your ex is all about facts and figures. Do your homework. Use the figures I provide in the other chapters of this book, especially in part 2, to show that your kids can be okay but that supporting them will require cooperation from the two of you. You might even want to bring with you — depending, again, on how positively or negatively your ex is likely to respond to such an approach — some quotes like this:

> Not to minimize the stresses and risk to children that separation and divorce create, it is important to emphasize that

approximately 75–80% of children and young adults do *not* suffer from major psychological problems, including depression; have achieved their education and career goals; and retain close ties to their families. They enjoy intimate relationships, have not divorced, and do not appear to be scarred with immutable negative effects from divorce (Amato, 1999, 2000; Laumann-Billings & Emery, 2000; Mclanahan, 1999; Chase-Lansdale et al., 1995). In fact, Amato (1999) estimated that approximately 42% of young adults from divorced families in his study had well-being scored above the average of young adults from non divorced families.[18]

If you're coming armed with statistics, come fully armed. You don't want your ex to hear a quote like the one above and respond, "Great. The kids are in good shape then. I don't think we even need these meetings." Come prepared to share the statistics on how harmful a non-cooperative co-parenting model can be for kids.

Enlist the support of another co-parent who has been successful: If you have friends or colleagues who are also co-parenting and having some success, ask for advice to help you prepare for the meeting. Discuss how to approach the meeting and what to include. Ask about their experiences in first establishing a good co-parenting relationship. Eventually, you may even want to invite one of these people to attend one of your co-parenting meetings to share experiences—but don't spring it on your ex at the first meeting. Wait until he or she is fully on board and committed to co-parenting, and until the emotional defensive mechanisms are just in stand-by mode.

Enlist an adult child of divorce: To help you prepare, find people to who grew up as children of divorce. Ask them what their parents did right and what they did wrong; ask how those decisions and actions affected them, positively or negatively. What was the biggest mistake their parents made? What was their wisest accomplishment? What worked, and what didn't? Be a good listener—ask questions, and dig deep. Take notes. Share some of these stories with your ex when you meet. In fact, again, at some point, with your co-partner's permission, you may want to invite an adult child of divorce to one of your meetings.

Pray! I saved the most important for last. Begin praying now for the right time and place to talk with your co-parent. Ask God to soften his or her heart toward the conversation.

CHAPTER 10

TEAMM Meetings

I wish I had a job of my own so my mom and dad
would stop fighting over money!
JARED, age 5

I was the spy and the mediator after my parents divorced,
but I HATED it when my parents put me in the middle!
I always wanted to tell them "It's not my job — you figure
it out" But I was too scared ...
ASHLEY, age 35

What do successful CEOs and Cooperative Colleagues have in common? Both manage — and sometimes even micromanage — their organizations in the same way: They are intentional about communication, planning ahead, and anticipating obstacles; they have a specific business plan; and they have a timeline for making decisions and acting on them. In a successful company, *nothing* happens by winging it — everything is done on purpose. Your approach to co-parenting, especially in conducting TEAMM meetings, should be the same. And your intentions should all come back to your acronym: The End Adult Matters Most.

Generally, though, the CEO of a company, although he has a big team of assistants who manage parts of the company for him, is usually alone at the top — he doesn't have a co-CEO who sits on another throne next to him. Your situation is different. You *do* have a co-CEO — what's more, you have a co-CEO for life! Sound overwhelming? I understand. But if you both love your kids, then you're both going to be part of their life for the duration; being a parent does not end at age eighteen or when child support ends. You will have graduation parties; you'll help move your kids to dorms and apartments and homes; weddings will come; grandkids will follow ... If you and your co-parent can get in sync *now*, the future details will be much easier to handle. I guarantee it.

Why an agenda?

If a CEO went into a quarterly board meeting without an agenda, he wouldn't accomplish much — which means he wouldn't be an effective leader. Not only would the board lose sight of the goal, but the CEO would flounder, get off track, and experience frequent frustrations, confusion, and distractions. For TEAMM meetings to work, the co-parents need to come up with a plan and then work the plan — and occasionally evaluate the plan to see if it needs modification. You and your ex-spouse, co-CEOs in charge of your children, have the highest calling on earth. You've been entrusted with priceless treasures. For the sake of those treasures, you need to suck it up and do what doesn't come easily.

Having an agenda at your TEAMM meetings helps in many ways. It keeps you on topic and makes it more likely you'll come up with decisions on the items that are most crucial. It also helps you keep track of topics for future meetings; if you begin discussing something but decide to table it for now, you'll have a record of it — and it can make its way onto the agenda for a future meeting.

John and I didn't start out having organized meetings, much less putting an agenda together. What I'm sharing in this chapter took us eighteen months of trial and error — mostly error. But we eventually came up with a plan that works. I want to save you that year and a half of struggle. Here's a shortcut: Start out with an agenda right from the beginning. You'll save yourselves a lot of strained communication and crossed purposes.

In the beginning, our meetings were usually one to two hours long, approximately once a month. We met at a restaurant for coffee or breakfast. We still do that; but when we can't coordinate schedules to meet in person, we connect by phone at an agreed-upon time in the evening after Angelia is asleep. Discussing these topics in private, with just the adults present, is the most ideal format for communication and problem solving.

That simple pattern has worked for our co-parenting team and for many other families. I pray it will open the conversational path for your co-parenting TEAMM meetings, too.

Suggestions for discussion

Below is a sample agenda for TEAMM meetings that I suggest as a starting point. Please modify it as needed for your own situation and for the ages of your children – the details change with every year. Our co-parenting discussions started out with potty training and what to do about the pacifier; we've now moved on to iPods and Internet use and dance and drum lessons. Don't get sidetracked by irrelevant issues just because they're on my list below – stick to the pertinent topics for *your* situation and *your* children.

Who sets the agenda? Don't get hung up on that. It's not a power play. Just make sure that *you* come prepared with your list of items for discussion, and encourage your co-parent to do the same. That way, you're each satisfied that your concerns have been addressed – as long as you both remember to not hog the microphone.

Here are some suggested topics. I've tried to make this list as complete as possible, so it undoubtedly includes many things you won't need to discuss at your first meeting, perhaps not even for years. If your child is five years old, for instance, you can breathe easy on the car-key issue for a few more years! (But your time will come.)

1. Children's Schedule
   a. School activities: teacher meetings, award ceremonies
   b. Extracurricular activities: sports, music, art, dance, etc.
   c. Upcoming holidays or vacations
   d. Other special events or activities coming up
   e. Parent travel or other conflicts – adjustments to schedule needed?

2. Discipline
   a. Current behaviors that may be cause for concern
   b. Current methods of discipline – What's working? What's not?
   c. Consider new consequences? Should they be consistent at both homes for serious offenses?
   d. Parenting books to read and discuss; other resources

3. Finances Related to Needs of the Children

4. Life Details (regarding children)
   a. School
   b. Friends and social life
   c. Emotional life: see any red flags?
   d. Medical and physical concerns: overall health, exercise, diet, physical development
   e. Spiritual life
   f. Extended family: grandparents, etc.
   g. Life routine: homework, bedtime, chores
   h. Internet use: how much, restrictions on content, etc.
   i. Other electronic devices: iPod, cell phones, computer
   j. Cultural media: music, movies, books
   k. Car: driving concerns, car repairs, budget for gas
   l. Other

5. Next Meeting Date, Time & Location:

Note: you can download this free document at our website and then modify for your specific children's concerns. See www.CoparentingInternational.com

Tips for Productive TEAMM Meetings

Eliminate the noise. When biological parents (and stepparents) are trying to communicate, letting unresolved issues and emotions intrude on the conversation is nearly always counterproductive. Intentionally leaving all difficult emotions out of your TEAMM meeting is part of being a healthy-minded co-parent. Some of those issues and disagreements will never be resolved, so if you hold your children's welfare hostage till they are resolved your kids' needs won't be met. The shared goal amongst the parenting team should be the well-being of your children and the preservation of their emotional health.

How often? Ideally, I think you'd want to have TEAMM meetings once a month. Can you get by with holding them less often? Yes, and if your ex is balking at monthly meetings, suggest quarterly meetings. That's a start, and it's certainly better than not meeting at all. In a year or two, when you've both discovered with relief that the meetings are safe places focused not on the two of you but on your kids, maybe you can increase the frequency.

> *Lead gently, don't demand.*
> *Explain calmly, don't criticize.*
> *Listen more than you talk.*
> *Seek to understand, not just*
> *to be understood.*

Save it for the meeting. Agree up-front to save your discussions for the scheduled meetings – and always have at least one scheduled. In the beginning, either John or I would try to call the other about issues in the middle of the work day, causing more stress. How much fun is it to get a call from your ex when you're in the middle of a crucial project at work? The likely result is that one of you will be stressed because you've got an important issue you think needs quick resolution, and the other will be distracted and annoyed – not a formula for effective and productive communication.

Be rested and ready. Schedule your TEAMM meetings or phone calls at a time when you're likely to be well rested, relaxed, and not hungry. For the coffee drinkers among us, be sure to be fully caffeinated as well. That way, you can bring your best efforts and your best self to the process so that your input will be as positive and helpful. Everyone wins.

Kids first! All parties should come prepared to work together for the best interest of the children – not to settle old scores or rehash ancient arguments. Think "Kids First!" and "Past Last!"

Teamwork is the ability to work together toward a common vision.
The ability to direct individual accomplishments toward organizational objectives.
It is the fuel that allows common people to attain uncommon results.
ANDREW CARNEGIE

This is my hope and prayer for you, your kids, and your co-parent at your TEAMM meetings: May you achieve uncommon results in those meetings so that your children will have an uncommonly stable and healthy life — today, tomorrow, and forever. It is possible. Yes, it requires hard work, but your children are worth every ounce of intentional effort. Pick up the phone and start the process of initiating TEAMM meetings for your kids before the next thirty minutes of life pass you by. The past doesn't matter — the future starts NOW!

CHAPTER 11

Creating Consistent Standards for Discipline

A child's resiliency is greatest when he or she can
bounce back into a stable and secure environment.
DR. ARCHIBALD D. HART

Children need boundaries and limits,
combined with a lot of patience and understanding.
You still need to be their parent, not their friend.
PAMELA WEINTRAUB, co-founder of Divorce Central

My guess is that many of you, when you read the suggested agenda items in the previous chapter and saw that I'd included some discussion items related to discipline, had a surge of anxiety. *We couldn't agree on an approach to discipline when we were married — how are we supposed to agree on one now?* Working with your co-parent could possibly be easier now because you can focus entirely on the kids and not on your other battles. The pressure is relieved. You may find that when neither of you have expectations of the other to fill some personal need, you can work well together for a shared goal.

Discipline can be a difficult issue to resolve between parents, partly because it's something most parents feel strongly about. And the differences between you and your ex that drew you to each other in the first place, that you found exotic and exciting, probably meant that you came from different family backgrounds — which more than likely had different standards on discipline. Someone raised leniently has a hard time accepting harsh treatment of her children. Likewise, someone raised with rigid standards and little room for error may see anything less as disgustingly permissive.

If those issues were hard to resolve between you when you were married, they'll still be hard. Divorce doesn't end your parental duties; it just complicates them. When you and your ex were still married and living under the same roof, you struggled not just with disciplining the kids but also with setting boundaries, deciding on appropriate levels of freedom, deciding on consequences, and all the other complications that come with raising children. No couple escapes that. Even if you were still happily married, you wouldn't find a one-size-fits-all "how to" for every child's temperament, every child's unique personality, and every child's needed discipline. What works with child number one may not work with child number two.

New parenting books are being written every year. Probably, while I write this book, at least twenty others are underway promising "new concepts" for how to raise great kids. You can read plenty of different ideas on everything from discipline to time outs, nutrition, sleep schedules, public education, private education, home schooling, college preparation, athletics, creative arts, computers, cell phones – and the list goes on and on.

The parenting issue is complex. Staying on top of it, especially in a co-parenting situation, can be tough. All the more reason to create a cooperative team approach.

Approaching Discipline as a Team

One thing John and I discussed, early on, at our co-parenting TEAMM meetings, was discipline. Angelia was only two when we divorced, so we were dealing with all the common experiences of any parent with a toddler. We tried to read books about raising kids, and we tried to find a common language to use with Angelia in both of our homes that would provide some consistency for her.

I was blessed to have a cooperative co-parent. The process I just described will be impossible for some of you reading this because your co-parent isn't interested in boundaries or in being a healthy part of the equation. Until that changes, you can still accept the responsibility to create clear boundaries and expectations for your children in *your* home. You can't control what happens in the home of your children's other parent, but your children will still benefit from your good choices.

Attending a parenting seminar at your children's school, either by yourself or, hopefully, with your co-parent, is a good early step in the process, helping you identify some of the issues and evaluate potential approaches to take. You may find other resources in your local community for support in parenting – seminars, workshops, support groups. Identifying two or three books relevant to your children's ages would be a great homework assignment for both of you.

Since you know parenting is a delicate issue for discussion, don't take a "shake your finger" tone in your TEAMM meetings. Instead, approach this as a team effort. Think you're a better, wiser, more patient and loving parent than your co-parent? Maybe you are – but if you communicate that, in either words or tone, you'll alienate your co-parent and undermine the whole effort. Instead, humbly consider the possibility that your co-parent may have the children's best interests in mind too, and could help you to do an even better job in this difficult role. With that in mind, invite your co-parent to brainstorm with you on how to approach consistent discipline between your two homes – and expect a good outcome. Listen to what he or she has to offer.

Don't get aggravated if your co-parent has very little to offer. Maybe he or she hasn't thought it through well yet. Just toss out some ideas, and then suggest coming back to it in a few weeks, after you've each done some research on what is out there. Suggest places for that research: books, live seminars, the guidance counselor at school, a local children's counseling center. You may like to read – after all, you're sitting right now holding a book. But remember that some, perhaps including your co-parent, would rather watch a DVD or listen to an audio version. This book is also available in an audio format if that might make it more appealing to your co-parent to explore. You know the many ways in which you and your co-parent are different, and how you prefer to find and utilize resources may be one of them. Try to be flexible yourself – open to doing something outside of your own comfort zone in order to move the process along cooperatively.

Remember our discussion about "parenting forward" in chapter 6? Discipline is a great area for parenting forward – for not simply reacting to the discipline issues of today but preparing for what's coming next. Believe me, even though Angelia is only eleven, I'm digging into books on teenage girls right now. I want to know what to expect – I don't want any surprises. (As if there were any way to avoid surprises in parenting.) A couple of those books are such great resources on raising girls that I've passed them along to Angelia's dad, and he and I are both reading through them and learning much. We're trying to stay *ahead* of her level of development, so that we're equipped to be the best co-parents we can be at every stage of the game.

Finding a Balance in Discipline

In discipline, as in many things, the pendulum can swing – from leniency and permissiveness to harsh authoritarianism and corporal punishment. And while a firm hand may be the best approach with some kids and on some issues, it may be ineffective and even harmful with other kids and other issues. How do you find the balance – the right approach each time? And how likely is it that your co-parent will see it as you do?

First, realize the importance of discipline. Creating boundaries for your kids communicates that you care. You don't want them to fall into the pit, so you put a fence around it. They may chafe at the fence, but they know why you put it there, and that reassures them. Realize, too, the value of high expectations for your kids: Having expectations tells your children that you believe in them and their abilities. Again, they may sometimes rebel against the music lessons, or your frustration at their unacceptable grades or surly behavior, but they know at some level that it's because you consider them too precious to settle for that.

When you and your ex enforce those same boundaries and support those same expectations at both of your children's homes, it's doubly effective. Being on the same page with your co-parent about discipline and about the "lingo" you use at each house to discuss and enforce it can be one of the greatest gifts you give your kids! Does that sound nuts? Just remember, once again: it's not about you, and it's not about your ex. It's about how you work together, now and for the rest of your children's growing-up years, to cultivate and create the healthiest young adults possible.

I can tell you, coming from a divorced family, that if my two parents had ever shown unity and a joint concern for me like that, it would have made me feel safe. To know that the two people I loved the most were on the same page on how to handle me would have been incredibly reassuring. Would I have rebelled against it as a teenager? Probably. Would I have been able to verbalize the gratitude I felt? Maybe not. But deep inside I would have known that those boundaries meant that my mom and my dad were standing guard to be sure I did not do something that might hurt me — and that they were doing it because they loved me.

Which issues of discipline you address, and how you address them, will of course depend on your children's ages and stages of life. But at each of those stages, the goal is the same: you're raising future adults who will need to know how to do laundry, clean their living space, see tasks through to completion, do dishes, cook meals, organize a to-do list, pay bills, be responsible in their spending, drive a car, get enough sleep, monitor their own time on the Internet, distinguish between healthy and unhealthy relationships of all types, have a strong self-esteem and a healthy sexuality, arrive at work on time, be dependable, enjoy a strong relationship with the Lord, be a loving spouse and healthy parent, and the list goes on.

If you're parenting a toddler, it's not realistic to have him start doing his own laundry; but you and your co-parent can each have him bring his used dishes to the counter after a meal so he has consistent rules in both homes. If you're co-parenting a teenager, you probably think an alien has taken over her body and the situation is hopeless. I assure you, it's never too late to start something new – you can even parent aliens. Put down this book, get on Amazon right now, and find a couple of good books on raising teens. Order two – one for you and (assuming your co-parent is someone who's comfortable with learning through reading, rather than, say, listening on audio) one for your co-parent. (The appendix on page 229 contains lots of recommended resources.)

At times, because of the disciplinary issue being addressed, you might want to have your co-parent join you in dealing with your children face-to-face. For your children, such a joint effort underlines the gravity of the situation. John and I have on a few occasions sat down with Angelia together to talk about her behavior. After his remarriage, John's wife joined us too. The three adults met first, while Angelia was in ballet class, to discuss the problem, brainstorm solutions, and come up with a clear plan for a consequence. After ballet, we sat down with Angelia and lovingly talked to her about our concern and the potential consequence if the behavior continued. Talk about wide-eyed! She looked at the three of us like we had each grown another head. I am sure it felt a bit intimidating to her to have all three of us there, but we all had her best interest in mind, and we handled the situation calmly and clearly. Angelia had no chance to work one parent against the other, no opportunity to be manipulative. We simply identified something that needed to be addressed, we addressed it, and then we moved on. And then, having handled effectively what we came to handle, we all went out for an ice cream cone.

Avoiding the "Pushover Parent" Syndrome

You're exhausted from the emotional turmoil of your divorce. You're a single parent, physically used up from all you have to do.

You're also sensitive and sympathetic to the situation your kids are in, vulnerable and unsettled and unsure of themselves. So the best thing is just to let them get away with things, right? You just don't have the energy to deal with it, and besides, what they need right now more than anything is just love and reassurance. Not discipline. Right?

Don't let being divorced give you permission to be passive and let the kids get away with everything. Maybe you're the parent who has only limited time with your children, and you don't want that limited amount of time to be characterized by giving them time outs or scoldings. I hear you, and I sympathize. But don't let yourself just become the "fun one" – the "Disneyland Dad" or the "Money Mom." Your kids need a true sense of structure and clear boundaries at both homes, no matter how much time they spend there. Kids need family rules and appropriate expectations. One of the worst things you can do for your kids is let them get away with everything while they're with you, especially if you combine that with bad-mouthing the other parent who does have rules and boundaries. You might as well write your kids a permanent hall pass to detention and destruction.

Being too lenient is a particular temptation when you're tired. Single parents are probably some of the most worn-out parents ever – we're doing the work of two people all by ourselves, without backup and without a net. Friends and family and even a great co-parent may be helping; but as a single parent, when you come home at the end of a long day, that's only the beginning of our most important job: raising kids. Yet somehow you have to do that while you're doing the cooking and the dishes, taking out the trash, mowing the yard, and seeing that the water leak gets fixed in the bathroom. You don't have someone to share the bedtime routine of bathing, tooth brushing and, oh yeah, doing the laundry so there's clean underwear each morning. Then there's grocery shopping, car maintenance, paying the bills, overseeing homework and school projects, and even just scheduling haircuts. No wonder we're exhausted! I'm getting tired just writing about it.

And who has the energy to punish a child or put her in time-out after all that? Who can summon the moral authority to take away the iPod and ground a teenager who will then stomp off to his room, slam the door, and not come out all night? Gee, that sounds like as much fun as pulling out my fingernails one at a time.

Regardless of how tired and overwhelmed you feel, keep steady and stable with your boundaries, consequences, expectations, and affirmations. Do it because your kids need it. Don't be a pushover parent — that's the recipe for creating a disastrous adult. Instead, defy the statistics, defy those who think you can't be a great parent if you're divorced. Show them — and show yourself — that you can! Show your kids that you love them by giving them boundaries and being consistent in how violations of those boundaries are treated. And if you find yourself in a situation in which you can't handle the kids alone — seek out your co-parent who shares responsibility for those kids.

> First we form habits,
> then they form us.
> Conquer your bad habits
> or they will conquer you.
> ROB GILBERT

Need motivation to tackle this tough issue? Close your eyes and imagine the future: A houseful of grandkids, with your own kids and their future spouses as the parents. The kids are healthy and happy, loved, secure — and they're being treated consistently and firmly but lovingly by healthy-minded parents: your kids. Your kids had wise and consistent discipline when they were growing up, and that gave them the foundation to exercise wise and consistent discipline with their own kids. And as you enjoy this beautiful scene, you can know that you did what you had to when you had to do it, even though it wasn't easy, and that now your beloved grandkids are reaping the benefit. Let that motivate you in your most weary moments to be a powerful, on-purpose parent!

CHAPTER 12

Including
the Stepparent

I love my stepmother,
I wish my mom would too.
MARYANN, age 14

My dad is always going to be my dad —
no one can ever replace him.
I wish he would see himself that way
instead of being jealous of my stepdad!
CHARLIE, age 19

Not long ago, I was driving down the Interstate when red brake lights flashed on ahead of me – in all lanes. Traffic was backed up, and we came to a complete stop. Accident? Construction? I couldn't see, and my hope that we'd get moving again quickly faded as, five minutes later, fifteen minutes later, we hadn't budged. There's never a good time to get stuck in traffic, but that's especially true for parents. I needed to pick Angelia up from school at six o'clock. I looked at my watch. I looked back up at the sea of red taillights. I seriously doubted that I'd be on time to pick up my daughter. And I knew that Angelia's dad was tied up.

But I had an ace in the hole. I flipped open my cell phone and dialed Angelia's stepmom. "Paula?" I said. "You won't believe where I am right now."

Paula readily agreed to pick Angelia up. No resentments, no recriminations. My daughter wasn't wondering why no one had come, and even if the traffic jam lasted three more hours (which it did), I knew my daughter was safe and warm.

What would have happened if I'd spent the past seven years

being rude or mean to Paula? That phone call would have never happened, and Angelia would have been waiting in front of the school for three hours before I could get to her.

I have every expectation that, when Angelia is grown, her memories of Paula from her growing-up years will be as pleasant as mine. Yes, I had a stepmom too. She was a great cook, and she always made my favorite green-bean casserole when I came on weekends. Sure, sometimes we didn't get along, but it wasn't because she was my stepmom—it was because I was fourteen and more interested in boys and roller skating than in sweeping up after my little half-siblings.

I also had an amazing stepdad, John. He was so fun and would always play with me when he got home from work. He would cook me crispy bacon on Saturdays and drive me to the outdoor basketball courts and make "crazy eights" with his yellow Volkswagen. I loved him and I still love him today. His parents are also a rich part of my family history. Stepparents can truly be a great blessing in a child's life story. And you can help to make that happen.

Or you can contribute to making those memories difficult for your children.

Adding a Stepparent to the Mix

Let's start with the obvious—the point that was abundantly clear to many readers as soon as I mentioned "stepparent." If you're right in the middle of your divorce, or just freshly through it, the last thing you want to hear about is the idea of adding your ex-spouse's new love interest to the parenting mix. Some of you already know who that person is, and when you look at him or her, what you see (rightly or wrongly) is one of the reasons your marriage broke up. Even those of you who've been divorced for years, and who have had a stepparent in your children's story for a long time, may not feel that you've overcome all the uneasiness in that relationship.

We have to address the issue, though, because however you view the appearance of that new adult in your children's life, your children don't see it the same way. Children want to be loving and trusting. They want to love and trust that new adult, that new "parent-type" person, whether they call them Mom or Dad or by their first name. Regardless of how long it has been since your divorce, having everyone together still probably feels awkward for everyone – for you, for the stepparent, for friends, and for school teachers – but mostly for kids. Even the most mature and positive co-parents can bump into unexpected awkward moments that no one saw coming or has a written script to handle.

Stepparents can be a positive part of the co-parenting TEAMM. And I'll go even further: If a stepparent is willing, they can be a loving and supportive person in your child's life – an extra person to cheer them on.

Even before your ex gets married again, one of the most wonderful gifts you can give your *children* – remember, this is about the kids, not you and not your ex – is a positive attitude about both your co-parent and the person he or she is dating. Remember the concept of the *divided self* we discussed a few chapters ago? Children of divorce live with a sense of being divided – pulled in two different directions. One of the ways to help counteract that is to be supportive of the other parent and kind to the person they are dating, and even more so if they should get married. Let your children hear you talking nice about them to others, such as extended family members, and in private, too. It's important. Your children watch *you* for clues about how to manage their own emotions about the situation, about how to feel about the new parent on the block. The kids watch to see if you're okay about it – and if you are, then they can be okay about it, too.

Uh oh! I just gave you a weapon, didn't I? If all you really want is to undermine the happiness of your ex-spouse's home, throw broken glass into the gears of their new marriage, and make your children's time in their home as miserable for all of them as possible, then you now know how to do it – just be aggressively negative about the new stepparent, and let your children hear you. Bad-mouth her appearance, her job, her hair, her cooking, her voice, what she says, what she does; imply that she was responsible for the divorce and try to enlist your children in your "hate the newcomer" club. It will work. Sort of. Your children may join the club. But YOU will have made them miserable. Remember, kids want to be loving and trusting; but you just made that impossible. And eventually it will backfire; your children will resent you for it. But hey, it'll feel good in a selfish sort of way, for a while at least.

Or, you can decide to do what comes hard for you in order to make things easier and better for your children.

What Makes It Work?

Let me suggest some of the "best practices" that John and I have used over the years that have worked well for us in incorporating stepparents. Are we the ultimate role models in co-parenting? No, of course not. But we've made it work, and some of the things we've done have worked well enough that I strongly recommend them.

Here's one: Our co-parenting TEAMM meetings and conference calls include Angelia's stepmom, Paula. Even when John and Paula were just engaged, I asked John to bring her to our co-parenting meetings because I knew that if my daughter was going to be with her dad 50 percent of the time, and if her dad was going to get married, then she would be with her stepmom half the time, too. In other words, she would be spending as much time with this new woman as she would with me! So it was clear to me that the best situation would be if all three of us were on the same page, working together as a team. I worked hard, intentionally, consciously, at being friendly with Paula in public. When Angelia and I were alone, I made it a point to even compliment Paula on many occasions. As I pointed out in earlier chapters, when it was necessary to address a behavioral issue with Angelia, the *three* of us consulted on it, agreed on the consequences, and supported each other.

Is that kind of teamwork possible for every family? Sure—if you have cooperative colleagues who are willing to *make* it possible. If your ex-spouse or the new stepparent refuses to cooperate, you may not be able to have the meetings – but your children can still hear your positive attitude, and take their own from it. Teamwork is possible, and it's best for the kids – even if it is awkward for everyone. This isn't a natural situation, and it doesn't feel like one. You'll have to *work* at how to handle it.

If our experiences in making a team out of not just Angelia's parents but her stepparents too have gone well, it's because we talk about it. A lot. Before any event at which we will all be present, we talk it out. Who'll sit where, who'll do what with Angelia when. All of those details are discussed and decided among the adults – when Angelia's not there to listen or observe.

For example, Angelia has been involved in dance for years. The annual dance recital in the spring is at a downtown auditorium with professional lights and production services – a big deal – and each year we plan ahead for weeks with costumes, makeup, rehearsals, and the ordering of trophies. (Angelia's stepmom came up with the great idea of the trophies.) We always try to agree before the event, as far in advance as possible, who will sit where, who will help Angelia with her costume and makeup, where we will take photos afterward, where we are going for a celebration dinner after – all of those "event day" details.

And why do we do all this? Our goal is to protect Angelia from anything uncomfortable or awkward at the event. On her big night, the last thing she needs is for the "grown-ups" to start fighting about where we're going to eat or who is going to take her home that night. What she needs is calm, cooperative co-parents who show up and smile at all of her events.

I even take a family photo of Angelia with her dad, stepmom, two stepbrothers, and stepsister after each performance. It helps Angelia to celebrate her entire family. It's complicated, sometimes a bit awkward, but extremely positive.

Way back in the beginning, I made it a point to be friendly and reach out to Angelia's stepmom. I didn't want her to feel ignored; I didn't want her to think I had any problem with her being present;

I didn't want her feeling so miserable or out of place she wished she were somewhere else. I never wanted Angelia to feel that she had to choose favorites or act differently toward Paula when I was around. I have encouraged Angelia to love Paula, and I have always spoken highly of her to Angelia. I once wrote Paula a note thanking her for something that meant a great deal to me. (Here's a hint: Paula's a nurse and much better at medical crises than I am.) I helped Angelia pick out a Mother's Day card for Paula, and on most Mother's Days, I've encouraged Angelia to call her. I have tried, as much as possible, to explain to Angelia that Paula's presence means she has one more person to love her. I don't have to be territorial or defensive. I'm not afraid that Angelia will love her more. Angelia's heart has plenty of room to love everyone, and I never want her to feel like she has to love someone else less in order to love me more or to gain or keep my love. Many angry parents seem to "threaten" their children with the idea of taking away their love if the child loves the new stepparent. Comments like, "Well, fine! Guess your stepdad can just replace me and *be* your dad; you don't need me anymore. I'll just stay away and let you have a big happy family with your mom and your stepdad." As childish and sarcastic as that sounds, I have heard that kind of comment before. I have had many children tell me about those kinds of threatening comments. All they do is create insecurity and stress inside children. Sarcastic comments will not cause a child to love you more; if anything, they will cause resentment and frustration to the point that your child may push you away even when you do try to love them.

Be secure in who you are as a parent. Don't let the presence of another adult in your child's life be a negative thing. Be the mature one; offer the bridge of positive communication. Encourage your children to be kind and respectful to their stepparent. In the long run, your mature attitude will convey a priceless message to your children. Finding creative ways to include the stepparent is a beautiful gift to your children.

When You Just Can't

I know that even reading this chapter has been difficult for many of you, probably causing a few tears, a few words you hope the kids didn't hear, and a few feelings of anger and guilt and inadequacy and bitterness. The simple truth is: In the cauldron of betrayal and failure and disappointment and grief that is divorce, some relationships, at least for a period of time, aren't going to be healed. It's useless to talk about whether they *could* be, if all the conditions were right, if the right words were spoken. Those conditions aren't going to be met, and the relationships will stay raw.

If one of those relationships for you is with your ex's fiancé or new spouse, then maybe the thought of the nice, constructive behavior we've been talking about in this chapter sets your teeth on edge, and you're muttering "No way!" under your breath. Maybe you feel you're going crazy each time you see that stepparent, and find yourself grinding your teeth. If that describes you, then do your kids a favor: If you just can't make nice, then at least *do not* express those feelings to your kids. Your kids know something is wrong there; they're sensitive to your feelings. Even so, be mature enough and love your kids enough to keep those thoughts to yourself. Find appropriate adults to talk to about all the things that drive you nuts. If at all possible, when you're all in proximity, such as when you're transitioning the kids from one house to the other, remain emotionally neutral—don't respond to your ex's new spouse with harshness or anger.

If that person speaks or acts with hostility toward you, don't respond to inappropriate behavior with more inappropriate behavior. It will just hurt your kids. If including the stepparent in co-parenting conversations is too difficult, then keep the TEAMM meetings between you and the other biological parent. Most divorce decrees require only that the biological parents communicate about life decisions for the children. Involving stepparents is a privilege for them—but if they can't be mature, then it's time to set some boundaries. The TEAMM meetings and discussions are too important to compromise. They must be kept productive.

The truth of the matter is, co-parents and stepparents can either find a way to work together or spend the rest of their lives being angry and conflicted at every important event. If that happens, then no one will suffer for it more than your children. The more you can include the stepparent, the better. If you're one of those for whom, right now, that's completely impossible, then your goal should be to work toward *making* it possible, whatever that takes — for your kids' sake.

One day, Angelia will graduate from high school, and when she does, her four parents will all be there, cheering her on. When she moves into her dorm room as a freshman, and then, years later, on her wedding day, we'll all four be there. Lord willing, the four of us will continue to be a great team when the grandchildren arrive — and everyone (especially Angelia) will have fond memories of each of these monumental moments.

When co-parents and stepparents all work together, cooperatively, the kids always win!

It really is true, as the famous proverb says: *It takes a village to raise a child.*

PART FOUR

If It *Can* Go Wrong …

When Your Co-Parent Won't Cooperate

No one can make you feel inferior
without your permission.
ELEANOR ROOSEVELT

I met Steve through my co-parenting seminars. His experience in co-parenting was about as far removed from John's and mine as you can imagine. After his wife moved out and filed for divorce, he emailed her and suggested that they set up a regular time to meet at a neutral restaurant – something they'd done a time or two to try to hash out the particulars of the divorce settlement – to discuss how to best parent their kindergarten-age daughter. He suggested meeting once a month.

After a couple of weeks with no response, he emailed again and restated his suggestion.

After a couple more weeks, he tried again, this time suggesting that if the idea of a monthly meeting made her uneasy, they should start with quarterly meetings.

Still no response.

So he emailed again and asked for her suggestions on how she would like to handle parenting questions, decisions about the future, and so on. No response again.

Eventually it became clear. As the custodial parent, she had no intention of any kind of cooperative parenting interaction. She and, eventually, her new husband, would make all decisions about the child. Steve would not be consulted or, unless absolutely necessary, even informed. And it was easy for Steve to tell, from things his daughter said (even though he was careful not to dig deeper), that the words his ex spoke in her home about him, even in front of their daughter, were harsh and accusatory.

When Steve found himself around his ex at school events or at the door at hand-off time, she was cordial but distant. Like me, Steve had decided not to make those times an occasion for negotiations or recriminations, so no business was conducted—and other than at those times, he almost never had the opportunity to see or speak to his ex.

A cooperative colleague she was not.

What do you do when, like Steve's ex, your co-parent won't cooperate? What if your ex seems to be out to sabotage you in your children's eyes? Unfortunately, this isn't uncommon—in fact, it's more common than not. After all, you're not married to each other for a reason. Divorces aren't easy or painless; people don't undertake them lightly. Clearly, either you or your ex-spouse had what you considered to be a strong reason for filing. And that reason, whatever it was, may still be making interaction between the two of you difficult. In fact, one or both may seem to *prefer* fighting to working together.

Remember the five categories of co-parenting we discussed back in chapter 8? Half of the couples in the study sample were either angry associates or fiery foes. So we can probably assume that half of you reading this book are going to experience some pretty strong resistance from your ex-spouse in putting together a cooperative co-parenting TEAMM—unless, and this is my prayer for you, you both see that continuing to fight between yourselves will just hurt your children more than you will hurt each other.

Tips for Dealing
with an Uncooperative Co-Parent

Things to understand

You can't change the other parent. Each of you has a unique personality. You each spent years developing from the genetic inheritance you started with. You may "clash"—but you can't change each other. Keep your expectations realistic so that you don't exhaust yourself with the hope of changing the other parent. If the two of you have a long history, you probably know this already.

You can't control the other parent. For those of you who are divorced or separated, you probably already learned this through the struggle that led you to the courts. You can't control your ex's words, actions, or belief system. In the years of experience you have with your children's other parent, he or she has undoubtedly done or said things that you didn't like. My guess is that your efforts to change those patterns of behavior didn't work. The best you can do is live your own life in a way that presents a constructive model for others, if they so choose. But in the end, people make their own choices, and you can't control anyone.

A tool to use

A powerful tool I've used in the past to reinforce the idea of how much continued hostility between the two parents hurts the kids is a DVD of a panel of teenagers that I interviewed – all from divorced parents, all living between two homes. One even shuttled between two states. I asked those kids a handful of direct questions about how their parents are behaving, and how that makes them feel.

Just to give you a taste, here's a sampling of the questions and responses:

- *What is the most important thing you want co-parents to know?*
  Peter, a senior at a private high school: When my parents divorced they were not friends, but you have to work together. There is a time to hurt and grieve for yourself, but you have to work with your other parent. When I got my car they both set the rules – same driving rules at Mom's and Dad's. For college they have both been helping me in the same direction. Not trying to turn one parent against the other. It has made it so much easier on me.
  Brianna, a senior at a public high school in an affluent area: I am

definitely guilty of manipulating my two parents, because they are *not* on the same page. It's easy to work them against each other, and I do that to get something out of them when I want it. I know that's not good and not healthy. I would actually, in the long run, feel better if my parents were communicating better — one of my parents will do something great for me but it is usually only because they want to show off and get back at the other. So I know they are not really looking out for me. I wish they were. It's like a big game, and I wish they would be more of a team.

- *To the oldest siblings: Were you the babysitter after the divorce? How did you feel about it?*

  Lucy, a junior at a small private high school: I became the mom when my parents divorced. My mom became very weak and grieved a lot. I took that as a sign I had to step up and be the parent. I didn't grieve for over two years because I couldn't. I had to be there for my mom. And I had to handle dinner, homework, and cooking for the family — my little brother and sister. I felt like it was my obligation. Now I resent many parts of it; but I learned from it. [When I pressed further and asked Lucy whether she resented her mother now, her very emphatic response: Oh, yes!]

I've seen many divorced parents change their attitude when, after watching this DVD, I ask them, "If *your* kids were on the panel, what would they say about how you are treating their other parent? What would they say about how you treat them? Would they feel like you were thinking of them first — or being selfish and rude?"

Does that sound harsh? I have a reason for asking hard questions of parents: I have yet to see a parent respond to those questions in a way that would indicate they don't care about their kids. They might be angry and upset at their ex, but underneath that anger resides a deep love for the children. Digging through the layers of hostility and hurt and grief so the core of love can shine out is the key. It might take a counselor or mediator to help you or your co-parent get there. Let's face it — your ex may not listen to anything you say. If possible, share the DVD with your co-parent, or ask a trusted friend to do so. (See our website for more information about the DVD. The same material is available in audio format as well.)

Tips for staying calmly on topic

Make it a habit, every time you know you are going to encounter your uncooperative co-parent, whether at hand-off time or at an event involving the children or at a scheduled meeting (assuming you've been lucky and skilled enough to talk them into meeting with you), to review these principles to prepare yourself for the encounter – and then put them to work for you, consistently, throughout your interaction.

Remain objective. You'll lose, and your children will lose, if you let your emotions get in the way. No matter what tone of voice or body language your ex employs, concentrate on being the one who stays calm and keeps your tone and volume down. Some people, and perhaps your ex is one, enjoy arguing and goading others into a confrontation; don't let him or her lead you into one. Keep your facial expressions neutral, your body language relaxed, and the tone and volume of your voice positive and calm. You already know that it won't be easy – in fact, it'll take intense self-control – so take a good look at your children and remind yourself why you're doing it.

If the meeting is an official TEAMM meeting, keep your language contractual and not emotional. Meet in public and use an agenda to stay on track. If your ex insists on bringing up other issues, just say, "I can see that this is important to you. Let's make a note of it and include it in a future meeting. But if we don't keep on topic, we won't resolve the important issues we came to discuss today." And then be sure to follow up on the other issues to build trust.

Similarly, **ignore peripheral issues** that do not have direct relevance to your children. Say, "I recognize that these issues are important to you, but they are not relevant to the co-parenting issues that affect Johnny. And discussing those issues will not help us find consensus on Johnny's needs."

Keep divorce issues separate from co-parenting issues. If the divorce is behind you, then let the already signed paperwork guide those details. Remind your co-parent that the only reason you need to continue communicating at all is because of the current and future well-being of your children.

Don't take things personally. Not easy, I know. What could be more personal than the well-being of your children? This will be extremely difficult since the very essence of your connection is related to your children. Give yourself a pep talk before each encounter: *I am strong, I am steady, and my ex can't shake me.* Choose a good friend to talk to before and after each meeting with your co-parent, so that you can vent your frustrations someplace safe — but in the heat of the battle, remind yourself to not take anything personally. Your ex may *want* you to take offense; your ex may *want* things to get emotional. "If my ex pushes my buttons, I don't think I *can* stay calm!" you may be saying. Reassure yourself that you don't have to remain calm forever, just when you're with your ex — which is a limited period of time, one that will soon be over. A half-hour later, sitting with your good friend, you can let loose. If you can pull that off — your children win big time.

Clarify boundaries. If your co-parent is hoping for reconciliation and gets confused by the fact that you're cooperating as co-parents, be clear that the positive communication about your children is not an open door to regaining a romantic relationship.

Leave the past in the past. Revisiting the details of the past is completely unproductive. Make sure that neither you nor the other parent get sidetracked on your mutual history. Keep your discussions current, and keep them centered on your children's best interests, current and future. If your ex keeps visiting your painful past, seeking clarification or wanting an apology, be vocal and frank — although kind — about your absolute unwillingness to do that.

Things to do when dealing with
an uncooperative co-parent

Use legal documents to your advantage. If you're divorced, you have a mutually agreed to divorce decree. Don't be reluctant to refer to it with your ex if he or she is not following it or is constantly trying to circumvent it in some way. Give direct reminders of what you both agreed to and both put your signatures to.

Bring in a third party. If the two of you seem stuck in an unproductive mode, you might need to see a counselor or a mediator to help you move forward in co-parenting communication. An outside, objective party can be helpful.

Don't fire back. When your co-parent is being hurtful and derogatory about you in the presence of your children, don't fire back. Later, on the phone or preferably in a meeting with just the two of you, remind the other parent that those being hurt most by such anger and judgmentalism are your children. Deep down, your children will be afraid that the hateful parent will eventually turn that hate on the children themselves. Your kids' thought processes will be something like, *Once I thought we were all safe with each other, but then the two of you split up and now you hate Dad [or Mom] and say lots of mean things about him [or her]. How long before you end up hating me, too?*

Know your rights – and your children's. Every legal divorce agreement (or parenting plan) I'm aware of clearly states that children are never to be subjected to derogatory comments regarding the other parent. If your co-parent continually ignores the agreement, seek legal advice. In some cases where one parent has proved to be a significant and serious threat, the court may decide that he or she cannot have unsupervised visits. This seems harsh, but the goal should always be the welfare of the children, and some adults are so lacking in self-control that they cannot be trusted to abide by the requirements of their own divorce decree. (See chapter 17 for more details.)

Agreeing to Disagree

If the two of you found it necessary to separate in the first place, then it's extremely unlikely you'll find yourselves always in agreement about parenting your children. Perhaps, before you pulled the trigger on the divorce, one of you said something like, "We agreed to bring these kids into the world in good faith that we would continue to parent them together. So how can we make a conscious decision that we know will not only deeply hurt them emotionally but will also, in all likelihood, throw serious roadblocks in the way of their continued healthy development? Can we do that to our own kids?" To which the other shrugged and said something like, "I need this divorce, and I'm going to have it. We'll just have to do the best we can under the circumstances."

Your views on life, parenting, discipline, education, extracurricular activities, fashion, friends, finances, and so many more topics are going to be very different from one another. Even traditional parents who live under one roof often disagree.

When you and your co-parent disagree on something, think carefully about which hills are worth dying on and which aren't. In the early months of the process, every detail will seem significant; but over time, you'll be better able to gauge which disagreements are worth fighting over and which aren't.

In the course of my counseling and teaching, I've talked with many co-parents who've had to decide where to fight – and where to give in or compromise. Here are just a few:

David and DeeAnne, divorced four years, have a son, Donny, who is musically gifted. Donny asked to take drum lessons, and David and DeeAnne agreed on a location, cost, and necessary supplies. They worked out transportation after school and agreed that Donny needed just one small drum pad which he could carry between their two homes for practice. (And that's a perfectly acceptable compromise. Sometimes kids take on expensive hobbies, and parents could go broke buying two sets of all necessary equipment, one for each house. Maybe one parent already owns a piano, and

the other doesn't. Remember: it's about the *children's best interests*
—not about using one's resources against the other parent.)

The next year, Donny turned twelve. He wanted to continue his
drum lessons, but he also wanted to take guitar and karate. Some
of his friends were taking karate lessons, and it was early summer
—Donny had time on his hands. David was in favor of continuing drums and adding karate—he himself had studied karate as a
kid. DeeAnne wasn't in favor of karate at all. She wanted him to
take drums and guitar, because she thought expanding his musical
education made more sense than his doing something completely
off course.

Donny's parents talked for weeks over the phone and at their
TEAMM meetings about the pros and cons, the costs and schedule,
the benefits and potential challenges. Despite the hours of discussion, they couldn't agree. In their first four years of co-parenting,
the two of them had split the expenses for extracurricular activities
50/50. This was different: DeeAnne refused to help pay for karate,
and David said he would not pay for guitar lessons. Ultimately,
after many difficult conversations with both parents struggling
for self-control, they decided that they would continue to split the
drum lesson costs—but that David would pay for karate entirely
and DeeAnne would pay entirely for guitar lessons and renting
a guitar. David was also 100 percent responsible to get Donny to
karate, even on the weeks Donny was with DeeAnne. The dollars
and time weren't equal, but they agreed to disagree—and they were
able to keep Donny's best interests in the forefront, and to keep
him out of the middle of their disagreement. The conversations,
though strained and frustrating, did not end in all-out war. Neither
called the other names or accused the other of anything. It took
about five weeks to talk it through and come up with a plan.

Another example: Rachel and Mike have two sons, three and
five. Mike had always assumed they would go to a private school,
as he had. Rachel had assumed public—she had excelled there as
a child, and felt that families such as theirs had an obligation to
be influential in the public schools. They had discussed this, with

some frustration, when they were married, but because the kids were so young they never came to a conclusion.

They divorced when the kids were one and three. For the first two years after divorce, the two boys went to a daycare hosted at a local church. The summer before the older son began kindergarten, Rachel gave Mike the addresses of two new schools and asked him to check them out. When he did, Mike found that one was a public school and the other was a home school co-op in the area Rachel lived in. Mike suggested they look at a private Christian school and a Montessori school—revealing a deep-seated disagreement about not only education options but another serious issue: finances. At the time neither of them could afford a private education for the children separately, but Mike had assumed that they would find a way to share the expenses, thus making it more affordable than when they were married and had only one income.

Thus began a long journey of interviews at a variety of schools and frustrating conversations about the pros and cons of each side of the education equation. A few times, they nearly launched into heated arguments about their differing opinions on the best option for the boys. Each of them, based on their own upbringing, felt passionately about their side of the argument. Each of them could make a coherent case for their preferred option.

After nearly two months, they reached a temporary agreement: Mike agreed to go with Rachel's suggested public school for the year. During that year, he would save money so that year two, if Mike and Rachel so agreed, their older son could attend the private school. In that case, Mike would be responsible for 75 percent of the tuition fees, and Rachel would contribute 25 percent. The three-year-old stayed at the church daycare.

Last I heard, both children were enjoying public school, and Mike has a nice savings account ready and available if they should decide to make the switch. Mike is very involved in the school and keeps a close eye on all the influences on his kids and activities they're involved in there. He's motivated by love for his children, and he really wants what is best for them. Rachel is appreciative of Mike's involvement and saves her own money in case they find themselves at another fork in the road. They agreed to disagree —and to prepare for a change if needed. They both love their sons and are regularly involved in their lives. I would say the boys are blessed!

Know what hills you are willing to die on
And don't let the smaller hills derail your journey ...

CHAPTER 14

When the Wheels Come Off

It's not how many times you fall down;
It's how many times you get up!
UNKNOWN

The co-parenting life can be a tough life, and it's not a question of *whether* you'll blow it at times. You will. Guaranteed. You'll blow it with your kids, your co-parent, and yourself.

In the previous chapter, we discussed the ways in which your co-parent might blow it, and how to deal with that. In chapter 15, we'll talk about the rest of the extended family, and the ways in which they can create problems. But this chapter is about *you*—about the times when your frustrated emotions override your common sense and you just blurt out—to your co-parent, or to your children—the first thing that comes to your mind, regardless of the harm it might do. This chapter is about the times it all becomes just too much, when you fall apart and cry in front of your kids, unable to hold it all in any longer.

People are not required to be perfect to become parents—in traditional families or in co-parenting situations. All you can ask of yourself is to keep moving forward, doing whatever it takes every day of every year to raise your kids in a whole and healthy way so that they will not drag, for the rest of their lives, the heavy baggage of their past.

What's Your Motive?

It has been a ten-year journey for John and me. We have both, at times, had to acknowledge to each other that we were wrong, or that we had not been patient in a previous conversation. We have had to agree to disagree on some topics, but in order to parent forward—to keep moving the ball down the field—we have had to work together consistently.

I appreciate John for his unfailing love towards Angelia. I know he appreciates my dedication and commitment to being her mother. We have struggled through hard conversations and complicated circumstances, and at times my frustration has shown itself as shortness, impatience, even anger. At times, he has done the same. Neither of us is perfect, and neither of us can be everything Angelia needs. Even so, we are committed to co-parenting her for her *entire* life.

It takes great humility to call your former spouse and apologize for losing your temper. John and I have both had to eat humble pie and apologize for getting short with each other. Sometimes it happens when we're trying to problem-solve something at 11:00 p.m., both of us too tired to even think rationally. Even when feelings run high, and you or your ex-spouse is upset about something the other said, you can get back on track.

A friend once asked us, when discussing one of our bitter disagreements: "What was your ex's motive when this situation happened?" It made John and I really think—not just about our *own* motives, but also about our *common* motive—to raise Angelia into the most whole and healthy young woman possible and to do everything we can to defy the negative statistics about divorce on her life. Although our methods may be different, and although our lives have diverged and grown apart, both John and I acknowledge that individually and together, we have the same motive.

It might happen at the baseball field as you're both watching Johnny in a game, or at Jenny's dance recital—something unforeseen happens, you disagree about how to handle it, and everyone launches into a flurry of frustrated, hurtful responses. Ask yourself, first and foremost, what was the motive behind that sequence of events? Most times – not always, but *most* times – I think you'll find that the motive was positive, but the outcome got messy because we are all flawed, imperfect people.

The motive may have been to encourage your shared children, but perhaps the words were clumsy, or perhaps the gesture was misunderstood by the other parent.

The motive may have been to protect, but maybe it was interpreted by the other parent as something negative, perhaps intrusion into the way they run their home.

Life happens without a pre-written script. When children are being raised by divorced (and sometimes remarried) parents, awkward situations will inevitably arise, usually accidentally. Certain moments will send even the best co-parenting team reeling.

Here's an exercise that may help: If you and your children's other parent were able to agree on one thing – what would that be? Think about it. Is there more than one thing? Probably. Here's some space to record your thoughts:

We agree: _____

We agree: _____

We agree: _____

We agree: _____

We agree: _____

Now come up with a statement of the shared motive – not just *your* motive, but the *shared* motive – that guides you *and* your co-parent in contributing to the raising of your children:

My motive as a co-parent is: _____

_____

My motive as a co-parent is: _____

_____

My motive as a co-parent is: _____

_____

Here's a challenge: Bring up at your next (or first) co-parenting meeting this subject of shared motives and bring a worksheet for each of you like the one above. Write down the similar goals you have, the dreams you have for your children, the future you want to create for them, the things you agree on that affect your kids. Clarify for your co-parent your personal motive in the co-parenting process. You have a common cause – take the time to articulate it and write it down. This will give the two of you something to come back to when either of you have failed. It will be a reminder that you share the same motive – and it can help re-direct your course when you find yourself in chaos. It can help get you back on track. This will, hopefully, give you a little more grace with each other when one of you fails at communications or is late to pick up the kids. Forgiveness and flexibility are key in co-parenting; they aren't easy and they don't come naturally, but if you want to succeed at co-parenting, you need them. This exercise can help.

Forgiving Yourself

More than anything, I want you to remember to forgive yourself when you fail. That is probably the hardest forgiveness to offer. Some people are convinced that it's impossible, that it can't be done. I don't believe that – it's far from easy, but it *can* be done.

Don't spend the next ten years dwelling on the past and all the ways you wish it could have been different. Don't surrender to a downward spiral of self-blame or negativity. Don't beat yourself up daily because you're divorced. Forgive yourself for being an imperfect human being and decide today that you are moving forward.

And do you know why you need to forgive yourself? For the same reason as all the rest of the decisions you make with regard to co-parenting: because The End Adult Matters Most.

When you're focused on your mistakes, on your guilt for getting divorced in the first place and for all the mistakes you've made since, you're clearly focusing on the past—on what's already been done and can't be changed. Co-parenting, or any kind of parenting for that matter, isn't focused on the past. It has to be focused on parenting forward, on moving the ball down the field—not on the broken play you just completed, but on the play you're about to execute.

> Honorable failure retains its commitment to start again.
>
> WES YODER

You don't look back toward the end zone you're defending—you look ahead toward the end zone where you hope to score.

So you ask God to forgive you and to help you forgive yourself, not for your own sake, but for your children's. And you encourage your ex to do the same. And then, as co-parents, you stay forward-focused. And when you fail, be willing to own the failure, to name it. Say "I'm sorry"—but never say, "I quit!"

CHAPTER 15

Filtering Out
Negative Voices

Become a "safe place"
for those you love.
DR. JOHN TRENT

What are your children's hearts worth to you? What price tag would you place on their happiness and success in life? What is their self-esteem worth today? What will it be worth in twenty years? What are the influences that are shaping your children's lives, both positively and negatively? Are you aware of the life-changing power in a single word, of the ability of those around your children to speak life to them — or death? These aren't idle questions, or rhetorical ones.

Stop and think about all the people who are part of your children's lives: your immediate family, neighbors, friends, grandparents, aunts, uncles, coaches, youth pastors, teachers, principals, and community leaders. If you had to write a list naming each person who is influencing your children's heart and their outlook on life, could you do it? Would it be ten people or ten thousand?

How well do you know the people on that list? Do you know their personalities, their habits of encouragement or criticism? Their faith? Their temperament?

Take a minute and write down the top ten influencers who affect your children today, making a separate list for each child if necessary. Spend a few minutes thinking about what you know of them, how you've seen them treat your children, what your children have said about them. Then put a plus or minus sign next to their name denoting a positive or negative influence.

Top Ten Influencers

1. _____
2. _____
3. _____
4. _____
5. _____
6. _____
7. _____
8. _____
9. _____
10. _____

What specific messages are your children hearing from those voices? What words are those voices saying about your divorce, about you, about your children's other parent? What tone of voice is being used by these influencers? Is what's being said appropriate for your children to hear?

You have a responsibility to be the "first filter" to your children's heart. As a parent who loves your children, you need to be very aware of every influence touching their lives. Can you control what your kids hear on the radio and TV? You can control what media your children have access to in your own home, yes; but they'll hear about other cultural things from their friends, and maybe even see and hear them at friends' houses.

> Words today, destiny tomorrow.

Can you control their peers at school? You can intervene in the case of abuse, such as bullying; but while they're outside your home, your kids will make choices about whom they hang around with, and your control over what goes on in those interactions is minimal.

Can you control what gossip or careless remarks your kids

will hear about your family from neighbors, or coaches, or other adults? Maybe not, but you can at least reduce it and influence your kids' reaction to it. And you can certainly strive to be the protective "first filter" on their behalf, especially for toddlers and school-aged children.

The Rest of the Family

Let's focus the rest of this chapter on one group of influencers in particular: your extended family. Because your family was familiar with all the players, and even had personal relationships with them, feelings of anger, betrayal, and bitterness often persist for many years after the marriage has fallen apart. Your children may have one parent who has suddenly fallen out of favor with half of their relatives. Or they may have relatives who blame one parent for leaving and the other for letting it happen.

Here's what Tina had to say about it: "Although I loved my grandma, she seemed to thrive on negative family gossip during Thanksgiving and family reunions. I remember hearing about the horrible things my cousin's dad had done and what a lousy person he was—now that he and my aunt were divorced and he was out of our family. I felt embarrassed for my cousin and wished someone would tell grandma, 'Stop using such ugly words and such a mad tone of voice!' But no one did, and I heard those same negative stories over and over as I grew up. Even when I was in college, her harsh bitterness persisted. Yes, I'm sure some difficult things had happened in my cousin's life. But I'm also sure that as our grandma, and the others sitting around her nodding and adding their own two cents' worth, made those disparaging remarks, they were wounding my cousin's heart. Those were the last things he needed to hear about his parents. The adults should have had the wisdom to keep that talk to themselves."

Harsh and wounding words can erupt without warning. Children enjoying the supposed safety of a family get-together can hear a bitter remark about their other parent and feel as if they have been stabbed in the heart. Remember the I Factor we discussed in chapter 7? Every word spoken about a parent is internalized as if it was spoken about the child. Children know they are part of their mom just as they are part of their dad, so negative comments about either parent can unsettle the children's inner world, creating anxiety and confusion that children don't have the language or the understanding to process. The damage to their own self-esteem inflicted by the words of well-meaning relatives (or, in some cases, not so well-meaning) can show up with disastrous effect in the teen and adult years.

The adults in your family should know enough to speak carefully in the presence of vulnerable children, but sometimes their own bitterness and anger blinds them to the vulnerability of others. That's when, as a parent, it's your job to protect your children from any relatives who would say harsh things about your children's other parent. As odd as it sounds, you need to ask your relatives to never speak negatively about the other parent when your children are present. To your relatives, that may sound like a bizarre request — after all, some of their negativity probably has less to do with their own sense of betrayal than with their wish to support you by condemning someone who hurt you; but you need to help them to understand that your own feelings are more concerned, at this point, with the welfare of your children.

> My grandmother can say more in a sentence than a college professor can say in an hour and a half.
>
> TINA, AGE 41

The first holiday visit Angelia and I made to my extended family after my own divorce, I called ahead and had a conversation with one relative. "I'm excited to come see you," I said, "and Angelia and I have been looking forward to the visit. I just want to let you know that I don't want anything negative said about Angelia's dad, and I don't want to make my divorce the topic of discussion at the dinner table." Absolute silence. I could have heard a pin drop. I waited to see if anyone was still on the line.

Finally, an answer came — the one I had expected: It would be impossible to guarantee that no one would speak their mind, that the subject wouldn't come up, and so on. But I stood my ground; I didn't waiver. I repeated my original request until, eventually, we agreed that this would be a visit without negativity.

Was I reassured? Hardly. When Angelia and I arrived that day, I felt like I was on eggshells. I expected, at any minute, to hear the questions tossed out where Angelia might hear them: "Why did you divorce?" "What happened?" I had no desire to relive all of that again—I just wanted to have a nice holiday with my family, and for Angelia to be able to get through it without having salt unintentionally rubbed in her wounds. To my relief, only one time did that kind of conversation begin, and when it did, I reminded my relatives that Angelia and I would leave if the subject didn't change immediately. And my request was honored—with great reluctance. We made it through the holiday without having to leave early.

I was proud that I'd had the courage to initiate the conversation *before* the visit, rather than having to confront the negative talk incident by incident during the visit. Angelia's heart was protected by my phone call in advance and by my commitment to not let anything reach her ears that would be damaging.

Don't get the impression that I'm negative about or untrusting of the importance of family in the lives of you or your kids—just the opposite. In fact, John and I agreed, early in our separation, that if anything ever happened to the other, we would be sure the extended family would still have a relationship with Angelia. If I died, he would help Angelia stay in touch with my parents and extended family. If he died, I would be sure Angelia had an active relationship with all of his family. We should *want* our kids to have a wide array of family relationships; that makes for a rich childhood. But we should also be diligent, as I was, in

> I have set before you life and death, blessings and curses. Now choose life, so that you and your children may live …
> DEUTERONOMY 30:19-20

making sure our kids aren't inadvertently hurt by the comments of those they love.

Can I control the whole world? Can I filter all the media that impacts Angelia? No. Was I able to control the opportunity my relatives might have taken to make disparaging comments about someone she loved in front of Angelia? Yes! And you can make this kind of difference in the lives of your children too. Toxic people and toxic comments are not healthy or helpful for our kids. Voices other than your own will speak into your children's lives — so as their parent and their first filter, you have to take the responsibility to filter out the bad and let in only the good the best you can.

Who are those voices speaking into your kids' lives? What are they saying? Make sure those voices are consistent with a healthy co-parenting plan, that they're contributing to a healthy emotional life in your children. If not, step in and protect your kids.

PART FIVE

When Co-Parenting Is Impossible

CHAPTER 16

Abandonment — Can You Co-Parent Alone?

When my wife left, I was in too much pain
to look forward. I was a basket case.
I could hardly tie my shoes ...
but I realized I couldn't undo what had been done.
I had to hold my head up and move on!
I had to get control, take charge,
and lead my children in healing...

MIKE KLUMPP, in *The Single Dad's Survival Guide*

C*o-parenting alone* — it seems like a contradiction in terms, doesn't it? Like jumbo shrimp. And it is. A better name for co-parenting alone is single parenting. If the other parent of your children simply abandons you all and disappears, you have no partnership, no help — and your children have no parent-child relationship with that other parent. He or she is simply gone, leaving a vacuum. Most of the other chapters in this book, which are concerned with managing a relationship you don't have, don't apply. You're a single parent, pure and simple.

Nights seem darker when we are alone. The silence, at times, is deafening. For many of you, the journey of the past months or years has included not just divorce and heartbreak but a dissolution of the team. The other parent has abandoned you and your children. You're a single parent.

A single parent, however, is still a parent. You have little lives looking at your smile every day as their place of safety and the haven for their heart. As bleak as your life may be, depending on how long it has been since your divorce, your kids need you — and they need to see you moving forward with your own stability. You may feel like a frail weed in a strong wind, but your kids need you to be, for them, like a strong oak tree with roots deep under the ground. They need to know that whatever storms may come to batter that tree, whatever winds come to strip away its leaves and perhaps even break off branches, those deep roots and the mighty trunk of the oak will not be moved, like the tree of Psalm 1. The storm only makes it stronger: the roots go deeper, and the leaves, when reborn, are even greener.

Single parents, you have the power, as the one parent in your children's story, to be a rock in your children's lives. If that makes you panic, don't. You are not THE rock—that's reserved for Jesus Christ alone, and he will never fail them. You, however, have a bigger responsibility than most to provide a firm foundation for your children. You may wish this burden could be shared; but be assured you can, alone, lead your children into a whole and healthy life. You've read all the negative statistics about the children of divorce and about the children of single parents—but you can defy all those negative statistics by gathering a support system around you and facing the future straight on.

Walk well with your children in the privacy of your household, and your children will one day step out into their adult lives with every important skill and asset that they need to succeed. Don't let anyone tell you that you can't do it alone; don't let anyone tell you your kids will just be another statistic—those are lies. Stand up against those lies, and work even harder to prove them wrong.

I believe, and I know from many adult children of divorce who had only one parent, that it is completely possible to raise amazing kids in a single parent household. If even one parent—you—can get your life on solid and stable footing and maintain a healthy mindset about who you are, if you can bring consistency and love to your home, and you can deal creatively and firmly with the issues and concerns that need attention, then you will still raise amazing kids—even without the help of a co-parent!

Does all of that sound daunting to you right now? Here are two quick reminders: First, even though you don't have an active co-parent, you're not alone. You may *feel* alone right now, but it doesn't have to stay that way. It's important that you begin to build around you, if you haven't already, a support team that you can turn to for advice—spiritual and emotional support—and occasional child care. Remember the quote I cited earlier: "It takes a village to raise a child." Begin building your children's village now. Think of it as your own parenting TEAMM, because its purpose is the same as a co-parenting team: The End Adult Matters Most.

And the second reminder: It won't always be like this. My friend Steve, in the months after his divorce, felt appallingly alone and abandoned. A single parent with a demanding job, he was lonely, heartbroken, and having a hard time making ends meet financially. In the midst of that, he attended a conference at which one of the speakers was author Harold Ivan Smith, who writes about recovery from divorce. Steve got Harold aside one night and told him his sad story—and Harold replied with a simple message that was nevertheless exactly what Steve needed to hear: "It gets better. It won't always be like this." Just when Steve was beginning to think that the rest of his life would be characterized by the heartache and loneliness he was feeling at that stage of his life, someone who had been there and who spoke with the authority of experience reassured him that things would get better. And they did.

And they will for you, too. It gets better.

Bruce and Levi

Let me tell you about a man named Bruce. He and his four brothers were between the ages of three and eleven when their dad abandoned the family. His mother, Betty, raised all five of her boys alone. Their dad was not a factor in their story at all—not financially, not physically, not emotionally. Never once did they hear from him after he walked out the door. And mind you, this was back in the 1950s when divorce was really a stigma! But Betty got creative in building her TEAMM—she asked her sister to move in with her, and together those two women raised five amazing boys. The church they attended in their community in rural Iowa came alongside this family. Instead of shunning the "divorced woman" and leaving her in isolation, as many churches would have done in those days, they got involved! The men of the church took the boys hunting and fishing. The pastor taught the boys how to carve and work with wood. This little country church became a community of support to Betty and her boys.

Betty recently turned eighty-three. All five of her boys are strong, godly men who have their own strong families. All five are prominently involved in Christian service or Christian business. I wish you could see the photo of Betty's eighty-third birthday, with her five adult sons gathered around her — all smiling, all thriving! It can be done — even if you have to do it alone.

Another story: I know a young man named Levi who has two beautiful daughters. When the girls were three and five, their mother decided that not only was she no longer interested in being married, she no longer wanted to be a full-time mom. She moved from Denver, where they'd been living, to a small town three hours away. The every-weekend visits she'd promised quickly turned into monthly visits, then ceased altogether. The mom no longer had anything to do with her two young daughters, to their confusion and grief.

Levi was devastated. Not only did he have his own pain and sense of betrayal to deal with, but every morning and every night, he saw the tears of his two little girls as they asked, "Where is Mommy? Why doesn't Mommy want us anymore?" He had no answers, and he ran out of excuses for his wife's irresponsibility. Fighting back his own tears, he would kiss them good night, having given them no real answers.

But Levi did many things well in that dark time — he kept going to work, he kept doing the laundry, he kept taking the girls to school and preschool, he cooked for them each night (sometimes it was merely frozen burritos or waffles, but it was edible and hot and it sustained them). He kept taking the girls to church, he kept paying his bills, he kept reading to them and holding them in his lap at night, he kept talking to other friends about his pain and agony, and he kept his little single-parent family moving forward.

One year Levi and the girls were invited to join his parents and siblings and their families for a trip to Hawaii at someone's timeshare. "I can't take the girls and go on that trip," he told me.

I was shocked. He was turning down a trip to Hawaii? "Why not?"

"Well, it just doesn't seem right to go there without their mom. We always vacationed together, all four of us. It just wouldn't feel right without her."

Frustration for him flooded me as I listened. I could understand that he was hurting, and that his girls were hurting — but still ... "Levi — you *have to* take the girls and go!" I said. "You and your daughters are still a family. Yes, their mom has chosen to step away — but the three of you are *still a family*. And families take vacations. Families have fun! Families go on trips with their grandparents, aunts, uncles, and cousins — and they play in the ocean!"

I'm happy to say that he did take the girls and go to Hawaii. His daughters, besides all the fun they had themselves with their cousins, got to see their daddy swimming in the ocean, laughing and relaxed, secure in their extended family. They got to see their daddy coming back to life! Those girls will always carry in their hearts the memories from that trip. Though the trip lasted only five days, the memories and the photos will last a lifetime.

Talking About the Absent Parent

If your ex has abandoned you and your kids, and shows no sign of returning, then you have a different task from your co-parenting friends when it comes to how you speak to your kids about the absent parent. True co-parents, when they talk to their kids about the other parent, are talking about someone who is still active in their lives — someone they see regularly. But for your kids, the absent parent is a memory, a face in photographs—not someone they see regularly, and possibly someone they'll never see again.

Still, your responsibilities are somewhat the same as co-parents. Remember the I Factor. Your kids identify with the absent parent, probably long for him or her, and may have idealized memories or impressions that verge on hero worship. They know, in some mystical way, that the absent parent's blood runs in their veins. The worst thing you can do is give in to the urge to speak bitterly of the absent parent. The urge will be strong —after all, the person who, after all the promises made, abandoned you to the work, the responsibility, the bills, the heartache, and ran off to seek their own happiness. It's natural that you're feeling some anger toward him or her; but this is not about you—it's about the kids. You will be wise to tailor your conversations with them about the absent parent

> *Out of defeat can come the best in human nature. As Christians face storms of adversity, they may rise with more beauty. They are like trees that grow on mountain ridges—battered by winds, yet trees in which we find the strongest wood.*
>
> BILLY GRAHAM

—because there will be many such conversations—to the needs of the children, not to your own need to vent. Speak to them in a way that breathes life into the hurts of their lives—not in a way that sows anger, bitterness, death. Speak words of life.

That's not to say that you need to speak untruly. Don't give them false hope. Don't tell them that Mom or Dad will probably be coming home in a few weeks if you have no reason to think so. Tell them the truth—if that means telling them that you don't know if or when the absent parent will return, if that means telling them that the absent parent left to marry someone else, then tell them that. But don't tell them *more* than you know. Don't give in to the urge to say things like, "He's probably remarried by now and starting a new family. I doubt that he ever gives us a thought. He has new little boys and little girls now. He's never coming back, and I'm all you've got." If you have no way of knowing, for *sure*, that such things are true, don't say them. And even if you did know for sure, don't give the kids unnecessary knowledge that will hurt them.

And never say never. Saying, "I don't think your mother will ever be coming back" is one thing. Saying, "You'll never see your mother again" is something else. People change, and minds change even more often. You don't know the future. Tell your kids honestly what they need to know; don't give them false hope; but phrase your comments carefully. Your marriage is no doubt over, but the absent parent may one day decide to re-enter his or her kids' lives.

> *Some days I look around and ask, "Why in the world do I have to do this alone?" But there are no good answers. And it's just tough. So I don't know why. Many times I don't know how. Maybe if we just keep doing the best we can, surely God will make one enough.*
>
> ANGELA THOMAS,
> in *My Single Mom Life*

If you're "co-parenting alone," build your support team, and fast. Start with your church and family and friends. Enlist your "go-to" friends as an extended part of your family. Find other adults to get involved in your children's lives and to create new and unique roles they can play to fill in the gaps. Remember that you're still a family. Your kids need for you to do the things that families do. Find the resources that address specifically the needs of single parents without an active co-parenting partner; many are available. (See my list of resources in the appendix for some suggestions to get you started.)

You can create a wonderful single parent family. You can fill your home and dinner table with laughter. May your home be a haven overflowing with love, and your goodnight kisses be many!

CHAPTER 17

When Your Ex Is Unsafe

I wish my dad had spoke up
for me when I was little!
JARED, age 24

What was my mom thinking?
Her drinking and boyfriends seemed
more important to her than I did.
I wish she had come to more of my ball games.
I wish she and I had been the "package deal"
instead of her and her boyfriends.
ASHLEY, age 30

I told my mom, when I was five,
that this was happening.
I guess she did not believe me.
LEXI, age 25

Thank God my dad
did something about it!
He is my HERO!
PAUL, age 29

Two Kinds of "Unsafe"

You read the comments of Ashley, now thirty years old, among the quotes just above. Let me tell you more. She was raised according to a typical post-divorce schedule: she lived full-time with her mom and visited her dad every other weekend and two weeks in the summer. The courts, especially back then, assumed that if the mother was alive and breathing, then she was the better parent to raise a child. Even now, although courts claim to be unbiased, the burden more or less rests with the dad to prove that he should get the kids—otherwise, the mom gets the nod.

Both then and now, it has not always proven true that the mom is more fit. Ashley's mother's life was so chaotic that Ashley basically raised herself; her mom was too busy chasing after alcoholic, abusive men to be bothered with raising her daughter. Ashley was a typical "latch-key" kid from seventh grade on. She came home from school, made herself a snack, did her homework, watched TV, and practiced piano. About 6:00 p.m., she would make herself a box of macaroni and cheese for dinner. Her mom would call to check in about then and remind Ashley of the chores she needed to get done. About 8:00 p.m., her mom would call again to say she was still at work and wouldn't be home for a while. About 9:00 p.m., her mom would call back and say goodnight—she was still at work. But she wasn't. Night after night, Ashley's mom was drinking at a bar, with one man or several. She would often go home with a new-found "friend" to spend the night, then try to sneak in quietly about 5:00 a.m., before Ashley awoke.

On some mornings, Ashley would wake up to find no mom in the house. She would get herself ready for school, make her breakfast, forge her mom's signature on her homework from the night before, and walk herself to school—not knowing where her mom was or when she would hear from her (this was before cell phones).

But those weren't the worst nights. The worst nights were when Ashley would cry herself to sleep because she knew the loud noises down the hall were the sounds of her mother being beaten. More than once, Ashley tried to run to the neighbors to get help, only to have her mom's boyfriend tell her he would kill her if she left the house. Whether alone or with dangerous strangers in the house, Ashley lived in fear. She'd have been better off and safer living with her father or another family that could provide a more stable environment.

And as for her father—where was he in this story? Did she talk to her dad about the problems at Mom's house? If so, why didn't he do more about it? And if not, could he truly not see how troubled she was? Was there no evidence of neglect when she came to spend time with him?

One evening just before Ashley graduated from high school, she took a deep breath, tried to quiet her fears, and told her mom that she wished the loud noises going on in the bedroom with Randy would stop so that she could sleep. Her mother said, "Don't tell me how to live my life! Randy and I are a package deal. I've had enough of this. I want you to be gone by the time I get home tomorrow night." So Ashley packed a suitcase, called a friend, and lived the last month of her senior year at her best friend Erin's house.

I'd like to think that Ashley's story is atypical, but unfortunately, some parents choose to spend the time they should spend with their children with someone else somewhere else. Maybe they hire a babysitter or maybe, as in Ashley's case, not.

Or what about the little boy forced to visit an abusive dad every other weekend? If his dad is the problem, who's taking responsibility for the boy's safety? Perhaps the father is physically or emotionally or sexually abusive; perhaps, like Ashley's mother, he's guilty of neglect. If the mother doesn't step in, who'll help that boy?

Carolyn's story reveals a second type of abuse: It isn't always just the kids who are in danger. Carolyn separated from her husband Rory because he was unfaithful and because he had hurt her one night, grabbing her by the throat and throwing her against the wall. He kept begging for another chance, but she stood her ground, wanting to protect both herself and the kids. One night he stopped by the house, knocking repeatedly, calling out to her from outside, begging her forgiveness. She let him in — to keep him from embarrassing her in front of the neighbors more than any other reason. Forty-five minutes later she was calling a friend to take her to the emergency room with a broken arm.

When people like Ashley's mother or Carolyn's husband are in your children's life, who is the greatest advocate? Who is watching for and speaking up about the pain in their life? Who is making sure they are protected and nurtured?

Divorced or not, custodial parent or not, you are 100 percent your children's parent. It is the job of parents to protect and advocate for their children. If not you — who?

Having to step in and take bold, drastic action to protect your own children from the other parent's abuse or neglect, or that of some other family member or adult, is the nightmare scenario every parent hopes they never have to face. Experiencing abuse yourself, as Carolyn did, is nearly as bad. But when those situations arise, ignoring them and hoping they'll go away is not responsible parenting — and things inevitably just get worse.

Signs of Abuse

Many people who are being abused do not see themselves as victims. And abusers rarely see themselves as abusive. People often think of domestic violence as physical violence, such as hitting. But domestic abuse also takes other forms — psychological, emotional, or sexual. (Please see the "Violence Wheel" at www.domesticviolence.org/violence-wheel/ for insightful help. This chart shows the relationship of physical abuse to other forms of abuse. Each "slice of the pie" shows a different way abusers try to gain the same thing: control or power.)

Domestic violence is about one person in a relationship using a pattern of behaviors to control the other person. If your partner repeatedly uses one or more of the techniques on the following list to control you or the children, you need to seek help — call the police, or a pastor, or an attorney:

- pushing, hitting, slapping, choking, kicking, or biting
- threatening you, your children, or other family members or pets
- threatening suicide to get you to do something
- using or threatening to use a weapon against you

- keeping or taking your paycheck or possessions
- insulting or belittling you, making you feel bad
- forcing you to have sex or perform sexual acts you do not want or like
- keeping you from seeing your friends or family or from going to work
- keeping you from seeing your children

Parental Alienation Syndrome

You may have never even heard of this form of abuse before, but my guess is that you can tell what it is — either from the name, or from your own experiences with it. Parental alienation occurs when one parent seeks to undermine the children's relationship with the other parent and deliberately alienates the children from that parent.

It's not rare, and it happens frequently after divorce. Is it happening in your family? Why not do a little research to find out? A great website for more information is www.ParentAlienation.com. (Note: women are just as guilty of this as men, and sometimes even more so.)

Know the warning signs

How can you tell if your ex is attempting to alienate your children? Here are some warning symptoms psychologists have observed in children suffering from parental alienation syndrome, according to Dr. Douglas Darnall, Ph.D. (author of *Divorce Casualties: Understanding Parental Alienation*):

- Giving a child a choice as to whether or not to visit with the other parent.
- Telling the child details about the marital relationship or reasons for the divorce.

- Refusing to acknowledge that the child has property and may want to transport possessions between residences.

- Resisting or refusing to cooperate by not allowing the other parent access to school or medical records and schedules of extracurricular activities.

- One parent blaming the other parent for financial problems, breaking up the family, changes in lifestyle, or having a girlfriend or boyfriend.

- Refusing to be flexible with the visitation schedule in order to respond to the child's needs, or scheduling the child in so many activities that the other parent is never given the time to visit.

- Asking the child to choose one parent over the other.

- A parent or stepparent suggesting changing the child's name or having the stepparent adopt the child.

- Using a child to spy or covertly gather information for the parent's own use.

- Arranging temptations that interfere with the other parent's visitation.

- Reacting with hurt or sadness to a child having a good time with the other parent.

- Asking the child about the other parent's personal life.

- Making demands on the other parent that are contrary to court orders.

- Listening in on the child's phone conversation with the other parent.

What causes parental alienation?

What causes a parent to want to damage the relationship of their children with the other parent at the children's expense? Intentions differ from one parent to the next, but psychologists have suggested the following as potential motivators:

- An alienating parent may have unresolved anger toward the other parent for perceived wrongs during the relationship and may be unable to separate those issues from parenting issues.

- An alienating parent may have unresolved issues from their childhood, particularly in how they related to their own parents.

- An alienating parent may have a personality disorder, such as narcissism or paranoia, which makes him or her unable to empathize with the children's feelings or see the way their behavior is harming the children. Such personality disorders may also make the alienating parent more likely to be jealous of the other parent's adjustment to the breakup and cause the alienating parent to have extreme rage toward the other parent.

- An alienating parent may be so wrapped up in their children's life that he or she has no separate identity and sees the children's relationship with the other parent as a threat.

What to Do When You or Your Children Are Unsafe

If the burden of action falls to you when either you or your children are unsafe due to the actions of the other parent or conditions in that parent's home, then it's best to know what your options are. Here are some suggestions:

Create a record of misbehavior

If your children's other parent is engaging in behaviors or communications that you perceive as a threat to your children or yourself, begin to keep a record of that misbehavior. That record can be as simple as a spiral-bound notebook in which you record, by date, the details of each interaction that causes concern. It can also be something as elaborate as an email blog that goes to trusted friends and your attorney.

The format is not important; what matters is recording the

questionable behaviors. Should the matter ever come to court, you can objectively cite ongoing patterns that are destructive or irresponsible, such as neglect or abuse (including verbal or emotional abuse). Including photos or other evidence in the records is even better.

Enlist a counselor

If you have serious concerns about the safety of your children in their other household, and those concerns are not immediately life threatening, enlist a professional. Find a counseling center for your children so that they can talk to someone about what's going on. (Just imagine how something like that would have helped Ashley, whose story opened this chapter.) Share your concerns with the counselor and see if they can get to the root of the problem. It's always a good idea to get another perspective, another pair of ears to listen to your children's stories.

Sometimes children from divorced families (especially manipulative teenagers) will make up stories and create unnecessary drama in an attempt to play one parent against the other. Sometimes the stories you hear from your children are an exaggerated version of the truth, when the truth itself doesn't rise to the level of something you need to be concerned about. Despite all that—if you hear something alarming from your children, sit up and pay attention. Respond in some decisive way. Don't let any of your children become another Ashley, looking back at the age of thirty and asking why her dad didn't step in to help her. Or another Lexi, who started telling her mom at age five about the abuse she was witnessing in her dad's house, and yet her mom made no attempt to investigate. Lexi is now twenty-five and married to an abuser herself—the destructive cycle repeats ...

Enlist a lawyer

It's difficult to discern when to hire a lawyer because of suspicion of abuse. My best advice is to maintain a good working relationship with your divorce attorney, keeping the door open to ask advice or referrals. The website www.FindLegalHelp.org has a national link to local bar associations around the country that can also help you find local attorneys. Another comprehensive website of free information is www.WomensLaw.org. This website has extensive resources for each state in the United States – and the information is just as relevant to men seeking help as it is to women. They also have a helpful list of national organizations that link to various resources around the country.

Get a personal protection order

A personal protection order, or PPO, is an order issued by the circuit court. You can apply for this at your local county clerk's office, and you don't need an attorney. The purpose of the PPO is to protect you from being hit, threatened, harassed, or stalked by another person. It may also stop someone from coming into your home, bothering you at work, buying a firearm, or finding your address through school records. It can also stop them from taking your minor children, unless visitation is required by the court. (The information in this section is taken from www.DomesticViolence.org. More information about PPOs can be found there.)

Who can get a PPO?

- People who have been physically, emotionally, or sexually abused, or threatened by someone they have been married to, lived with, have a child with, or dated. Some examples may include: a current or former spouse, family member, partner, co-parent, current or former roommate, or current or former boyfriend/girlfriend.

- People who have been stalked. Stalking is repeated harassment that makes another person feel scared or upset. A stalker can be a stranger or a familiar person. Stalkers often bother people by giving unwanted attention – through unwanted phone calls or gifts, by following, or by going to the other person's home or place of work. Stalkers can also be threats to you or your family.

What should I bring?

- A letter telling the court what has been going on. Make sure to tell them everything. Include dates and details the best you can (record of misbehavior as noted earlier).

- Police reports, medical records, photographs, or witnesses if you can get them.

- Any information about the abuser you have – current address, date of birth or age, hair color, eye color, height, weight, address, Social Security number, or driver's license number.

- Any court papers you have if you can get them. For example, custody and/or parenting time orders, lease agreement, divorce papers, or criminal case records.

Visitation. Even if the abuser has a court order saying that he or she can see the children, that doesn't mean you have to let the person come into your home. You have other options: You can have a friend or family member pick up and drop off the children. You can make the exchange at a police station or other public place. Or, when you file your PPO, you may ask for supervised parenting time through the court.

Carry a copy of your PPO with you at all times. If there is a violation of the PPO and you need help from the police, having a copy with you to hand them will help them enforce it.

Prepare a safety plan

If you think you or your children may be in danger, a critical and comprehensive resource for you is the National Coalition Against Domestic Violence. One of the most proactive and healthy things you can do is to create for yourself (even if there is no overt abuse happening at present, as far as you know) a Safety Plan. Preparing this plan helps you think through boundaries you may need to establish for yourself and your children, and helps you think through how to prepare yourself for the danger you suspect may present itself. The plan that follows is taken from the Coalition's website, www.ncadv.org.

My Personal Safety Plan

The following steps are my plan for increasing my safety and preparing to protect myself in case of further abuse.

Although I can't control my abuser's violence, I do have a choice about how I respond and how I get to safety. I will decide for myself if and when I will tell others that I have been abused, or that I am still at risk. Friends, family, and co-workers can help protect me, if they know what is happening, and what they can do to help.

To increase my safety, I can do some or all of the following:

1. When I have to talk to my abuser in person, I can:

   _____

2. When I talk to my abuser on the phone, I can:

   _____

3. I will make up a "code word" for my family, co-workers, or friends, so they know when to call for help for me. My code word is:

   _____

4. When I feel a fight coming on, I will try to move to a place that is lowest risk for getting hurt such as:

   _____

   or (at work): _____

   or (at home): _____

   or (in public): _____

5. I can tell my family, co-workers, boss, or a friend about my situation. I feel safe telling the following people:

   _____

6. I can use an answering machine or ask my co-workers, friends, or other family members to screen my calls and visitors. I have the right to not receive harassing phone calls. I can ask:

   _____

   to help screen my (home) (work) phone calls.

7. I can keep my cell phone with me at all times. I can call any of the following people for assistance or support if necessary, and can ask them to call the police if they see my abuser bothering me:

friend: _____

relative: _____

co-worker: _____

counselor: _____

or shelter: _____

8. When leaving work, I can:

_____

_____

9. When walking, riding, or driving home, if problems occur, I can:

_____

_____

10. I can attend a support group for women who have been abused.

11. Telephone numbers I need to know:

NATIONAL DOMESTIC VIOLENCE HOTLINE: 1-800-799-7233

Local Police/Sheriff's Department: _____

Probation Officer
    (of children or co-parent if applicable): _____

Domestic Violence/
    Sexual Assault Program: _____

Counselor: _____

Clergy Person: _____

Attorney: _____

Conclusion

The motive behind this entire book is to encourage cooperative co-parenting. This chapter about possible dangers from your children's other parent certainly doesn't lend itself to a sense of cooperation; but I've included it because, unfortunately, some of you are attempting to co-parent with someone who is unhealthy and unreasonable. Your co-parent's instability may be due to mental illness, a troubled past, or drug or alcohol dependency. Whatever the circumstance, please remember that your first and highest commitment is to your children. God has entrusted these priceless treasures to you to protect, nurture, love—and to set free one day to soar into their independent lives. But they're not independent yet. While they are still young, you are accountable for them. While they are under eighteen, you have a say.

Please don't abuse the information in this chapter. Don't create problems for the sake of getting even. Don't make accusations without substance for the sake of gaining control. Don't try to get even with your ex by taking the kids away because you are mad. Don't do *anything* out of selfishness or anger, but do *all things* out of love and a stable mind.

I hope that most of you see no issues of concern or abuse in your co-parenting equation. I hope that most of you are confident that when your children are with their other parent they are safe —safe emotionally, mentally, and physically. *However*—if that's not the case, if you have *any* hints or clues that something unsafe is going on, then get off the couch and make a phone call. Don't be afraid to rock the boat. Find a kids' counselor and get your children in there this week. If money is tight, then instead of going to the movies with the kids, take your kids to a counselor, or ask your church (or some likely church, if you don't have a home church) to help you. Ask the guidance counselor at your children's school to get involved. The resources are there. You are accountable to use them.

Don't let your children grow up to say to you later in life, "I told you. Why didn't you do anything?" Instead, be like Paul's dad in one of this chapter's opening quotes, who stepped in and became his advocate, his defender, and his hero! Be a parent who says, "Not on my watch! No son (or daughter) of mine will be wounded this way. I won't allow it." May you find the strength to be brave, and may you find the support to help you clarify the unknown. Your children will thank you. Your grandchildren will benefit. And your conscience will be at peace when you lie down at night.

Be proactive!

Be protective!

Speak up!

Not on my watch!

PART SIX

Moving On with Your Life

CHAPTER 18

Dating Again

Wait for GREAT!
TAMMY DAUGHTRY

A few years ago I was at a meeting with some friends who are in business together. We met at Starbucks to talk over coffee, and I noticed there was an empty chair beside me. It made me a bit sad that I was there, alone, and there they were, together. I talked to my friend, Jana, later that day about the "empty chair" and how I longed to have a life partner to work with. I hated going to meetings alone and not having someone to brainstorm with and work with on all the projects I felt called to. Jana was kind and gentle in her response, and about a week later she sent me a fun little, Barbie-sized, wooden chair. The little chair was handpainted with fun zebra colors, pink border, and across the seat of the chair she wrote one word, "Hope." With it, was a handwritten note including the Scripture of Jeremiah 29:11: "For I know the plans I have for you, says the Lord. Plans for hope and for a future." Jana said she would keep praying for God to send me a life companion and that in the meantime she would "keep the popcorn popping," Jana's way of saying she would keep listening to my life story as it unfolds.

Three years later, the night before my wedding, Jana presented me with a precious gift. I almost melted into a pile of happy tears when she told me to open my eyes! It was a life-size, beautiful wooden chair with seven words painted on the seat: "Jay, Tammy, Angelia, Jaron, Jenna, Amanda, Hope." I had practically forgotten the situation from three years prior when I shared the "empty chair" story with Jana. Jana never forgot. Jana prayed and walked every day with me through the various journeys of dating and ate a whole lot of popcorn as we waited for God to bring Jay into my life. She is, by the way, one of those "go-to friends" that I have called many times when I needed her.

God turned my "empty chair" into a "chair of HOPE"!

Dating after divorce can be exciting and terrifying; but you wouldn't be reading this book if you didn't have children—and when children are involved, it's important to act wisely in order to protect their hearts. Life for the single parent is no longer simple and carefree. It takes intentional planning and wisdom to create a life of stability for yourself and your children, and dating again can certainly rock that world.

When is it okay to start dating again? When is it the right time to introduce the kids to the new person? Does the co-parent deserve an explanation? Let's look at some of the complications dating will introduce into your life.

Before You Even Think about Dating

What's your first-year focus? For the first year after divorce, focus on the health of your heart and the health of your children. You need time to grieve and to heal. No matter who filed for the divorce, and no matter how "over it" you think you are, everyone needs time to grieve. It's important to grieve the death of a dream, the death of the idea of family, and the death of the marriage. Let yourself process all of this—and allow enough time to process it thoroughly—before dating someone new. Attending a Divorce-Care class or a monthly counseling session will aid your healing far more than jumping into dating will. Surround yourself with healthy friendships that have no ulterior motives. Allow God to comfort you and fill the empty places.

The number-one most common mistake after divorce is that people jump immediately into a rebound relationship. These relationships rarely last. If you give yourself a year or even two to just heal, this will be the best gift you give yourself—and your children.

Only separated? Forget it. Please don't date during separation. Do nothing about dating until the divorce is final. First, it is unethical to date while you are still legally married. Second, it is unfair to the person you're dating – getting them mixed up in the messy journey of your divorce. The post-divorce personality is usually not a pretty picture, and dealing with your own emotions, disappointments, and grief *before* dating is the best thing you can do for yourself and your children, as well as for the new romantic interest. Third, dating while separated complicates decisions about the children and how much time they're allowed to see each parent. Keep your focus on your children; make being a solid parent for them your priority. You'll have plenty of time in the future to date. First things first.

Figure out first what you did wrong. No matter who insisted on the divorce, you were part of the marriage that failed. You need to come to grips with your own contributions to the failed marriage before getting involved with someone new. Since the divorce rate increases to 75 percent for second marriages, the odds are against you. Before you start dating, know what you could have done better in marriage number one. Go to counseling. Ask yourself and friends who knew you well what you could have done differently and better. When you've identified the areas where you contributed to the decline of the marriage, make a plan for how you're going to learn to do better. Attend discussion groups; read books.

Try a "God Date" first. Here's something you can do while separated and during that long, hard first year. When I was first single again, I decided to go on a date with God. We went to dinner and a movie; and when I got home, I wrote in my journal and talked with God about how much I enjoyed being with just him.

To all observers, of course, I didn't look like I was on a date at all – I looked like I was all by myself. That's okay, though. Sitting alone in a restaurant is something I encourage all single parents to conquer – as awkward as it may feel at first. And going to a movie, even by yourself, is great comic relief (or big excitement, if you're into action/adventure) and a lot cheaper than therapy.

Have you been feeling empty since you've been living alone? Allow God to fill your emptiness. In many ways, the bleakness of post-divorce life is where the rubber meets the road. It was easy to talk about trusting God back when you were safely married and surrounded by voices and people day in and day out. It's a lot harder when you're living alone, missing your kids and your ex, surrounded by S-I-L-E-N-C-E. Spend time with God. Read the Bible, listen to worship music, participate in group Bible studies, attend Christian conferences – allow your heart to heal and come back to life.

Preparing to Date

What's your motive for dating? Before you take the first step out the door on a date, figure out why you're doing it. Are you afraid of being alone? Are you dating just to make your ex jealous? Make sure before you invite somebody of the opposite sex to the local college football game that you are a healthy-minded and stable whole person, not an anxious empty person who needs someone else to complete you. That's only a recipe for disaster. Loving God and letting him love you back is the best gift you can give yourself and any future dating partner. That way, you can date someone because you want to – not because you need to.

Be aware of your own vulnerability. Most people feel discouraged and struggle with self-esteem during and after a divorce. "Am I pretty enough?" "Do I have what it takes to attract a new partner?" "Will anyone ever love me again?" Because of all of those questions about your own desirability, both physical and social, you may feel drawn into relationships as a way of answering those questions; if someone finds you attractive enough to date, then you can't be that bad. You're vulnerable, whether you know it or not. Be aware of that, and move slowly into dating. Too many broken hearts are created by hurting people who jump into serious relationships way too early as a way of reassuring themselves that they are lovable.

Create a "Top Ten List" – and don't settle for less. When you really think you've reached the point of being ready to date, write down a top ten list: the top ten qualities and characteristics you're looking for in a potential dating partner. Now study it. Are some qualities nice-to-have but not need-to-have? Are some non-negotiable? If so, stick to your guns – don't settle!

Getting Back in the Game

Group date. Explore the idea of group dating as a way to get to know each other. At least once a month, plan a group date or double date, and be open to feedback from your friends. They will be more objective than you, helping you think clearly. I've been fortunate enough to have had that kind of feedback from friends along the way, friends who were brave enough to speak to me with both truth and love. I didn't always want to hear what they had to say, but I listened – because I knew they loved me and wanted the best for me. I'm grateful for their feedback.

I give credit to one friend, especially, for challenging me to let go of the *good* and wait for the *great*. Sometimes our friends know us better than we know ourselves. Group dates will help us navigate these treacherous waters.

Accountability. Remember those three "go-to" friends you listed back in chapter 3? Here's another place they can come in handy. Ask them to be your sounding boards about dating – extra eyes to help you see what you might not see yourself. Ask them to hold you accountable to keep purity a priority. Don't wait until your first post-divorce kiss to decide how far is too far. My suggestion – no sex until marriage. I truly believe God's design is the best! Be clear with anyone you're dating – *before* the first kiss – where you stand on the issue of purity. If the other person does not want to continue dating for that reason, be thankful you discovered his or her character now. Although your body may feel frustration, so much more is at stake now than when you dated as a childless person, a lifetime ago.

The old saying, "True love waits" is completely true. Someone who loves you will wait. Trust God while you wait. Ask your friends to hold you accountable to your commitment – to God, to yourself, and to your children.

Do not discuss your dating life with your kids – no matter how old they are. They are not to be your closest confidant or companion or counselor. Find appropriate adults to talk to about dating.

You're a "package deal." Always remember that your kids come first right now. Unfortunately, sometimes lonely parents think more about their desire to date than about their children's needs. Remember Ashley, whose mom told her, regarding her boyfriend, "We are a package deal" – and then kicked her own daughter out? Turn that story on its head – tell your date, "My kids and I are a package deal." Never make your new dating partner a priority over your children. If you date someone who has no children of their own, be very certain they're excited about *your* children.

A friend of mine dated a single, childless guy – we'll call him Dan. She and Dan had a great relationship for six months. Then she introduced him to her children. One Saturday, they were spending the day with the kids and Dan seemed annoyed. When she asked what was wrong, he said, "I'm just sick of babysitting. All we've done today is babysit your kids, and I'm tired of it." My friend knew instantly that he was not the right one for her to date; being a parent was a full-time part of her life, and her heart was completely committed to her children. For her, being with her kids wasn't babysitting – it was parenting. Her relationship with Dan ended that weekend; and although she was sad, it was clear that he was not what she was looking for.

But not all never-marrieds are like Dan. Some would absolutely love your children. God knows who will be the best fit for your family. Be patient, and don't jump in deep with anyone too fast. Being a "package deal" will be great news to the right person. Keep your eyes and heart focused on God, and let him lead every step of the way.

Have you healed? Has he/she healed? Is the person you are considering dating healed from their own past if they too have been divorced? If God wants the two of you together, he'll keep you both until the time is right. Protect yourself and your children from someone else's baggage. When *you're* at a stable and healthy place, find someone else who's stable and healthy too before you dive into a relationship. The first year is important for healing — not dating.

Know when to end a relationship. When you know that a dating relationship just isn't the right fit, end it. No matter how much you have in common. The more prolonged the relationship, the more difficult breaking it off will be on yourself — and especially on the children, if they've already begun to bond with your date. One of my friends told me once, "You need to end this relationship so God can bring you the right one — and bring *him* the right one. The longer you prolong it, the harder it will be for God to bless you *both* with the right relationship."

Ending a relationship takes guts. Being able to trust God with the "blank canvas" of what comes next takes great faith. I've been guilty, I confess, of prolonging the inevitable. I can testify, however, that God will bless your obedience to trust him. He will lead and protect your heart. If you let go of "good" God will bring you "GREAT!" Those were three words God told me several times in my dating experiences: "Wait for GREAT!" I encourage you to "Wait for Great" and never settle for good.

When It Starts to Feel Like More Than Just Dating

When do I tell my co-parent? Some of you read that first line and immediately thought, *Since when do I need my ex-spouse's permission for how I conduct my private life?* I'm not saying you do. There's a big difference between informing your co-parent about something that affects them and asking for their input and approval. Anything that affects your shared children — and when either you or your ex start to date again, that definitely affects the children – affects both you and your ex-spouse.

It's also a good idea to inform your co-parent about the person you are dating before you introduce that person to your children. Your children may seem to you to be ready to meet someone new, but they might not be as ready as you think. This is a big step, and kids differ greatly in how they respond to it. Be courteous, for the sake of your children, and alert their other parent before the big introduction happens so that the other parent can be prepared if your children get upset.

On the other hand, your children might not be upset at all; they might be very happy to meet someone you're dating. And they might go to their other parent's house talking excitedly about it. Kids have a funny way of bringing up the most awkward information at the most unexpected times. If a mom or dad responds in hostility to the unexpected news of the other parent dating again, the children may get caught in the crossfire of unfiltered comments or emotions. Do your kids a favor and inform their other parent *before* you introduce the children to someone you are dating.

And when the time comes to consider marriage, be considerate of your children by informing their other parent of this news as well. These life transitions will impact your children deeply, and the other parent can be a sounding board for them. Hopefully, your co-parent will reciprocate by informing you of any significant changes in their life, and you can be the one to help the children with the transition.

I realize that this will be painful for many of you, especially if you're among the 50 percent who didn't want the divorce to begin with. Just remember: It's about the kids. Keep your focus on them, helping them get through these transitions with as much stability as possible.

When do I introduce the kids? Children of divorce have already experienced multiple losses – don't allow your desire for companionship to overshadow the wisdom that experts give on this topic. It might not be convenient or easy to keep the kids from meeting your new friend, especially if you're a woman and your new friend expects to pick you up at your home for dates; but it's not fair to bring the children into the relationship too soon. The last thing they need is another person to come and go from their world. Avoid the "revolving door" by not introducing kids to your romantic interest until six to nine months into the relationship – and then only if you feel this could be someone you might marry. This approach has a side benefit for both you and your kids: when you're with them, it will be just you and the kids, and you can be fully focused on them. When they're at the other parent's house, use that as dating time.

Romantic affection – setting boundaries around the children. This is a vitally important question – don't just wing it. Decide ahead of time what you feel is appropriate to express in front of your children. Your children will react to seeing you express affection and receive affection from someone new. Be sensitive to their feelings and save the romance for when they are away. Go slow around the kids; give them time to get to know the other person. Kids often get very territorial about their parent. If they feel jealous, or if they sense that you are paying more attention to your new date than to them, they may react with such tactics as trying to squeeze between you when you hug, or shoehorn themselves between the two of you as you're sitting on the couch.

And remember, especially for the older kids, you are modeling dating. The kids will follow your example. What patterns do you want them to follow? You want everything your children observe in you and your date now to be exactly what you would hope for their dating life one day. This is an odd part of being a single parent and dating again. Don't compromise or get lazy about appropriate boundaries. Model well.

What is their co-parenting relationship with their former spouse? If you're divorced, then in all likelihood the vast majority of people in your "dating pool" will be divorced or widowed. When you date someone with children, be wise: Look at the bigger picture – not just who this person is when he or she is with *you,* but who he or she is in relationship with others. How does he talk about his former spouse? If you've progressed to the point of meeting her kids, what does she say about her former spouse in front of her children? Is he still stuck in unresolved anger? Does she put her kids in the middle? (These would all be red flags, because those issues would become major problems if you were to marry this person.) If you marry someone with children, you marry into his or her family equation, and that includes the ex who will forever be a co-parent to your stepkids. (And we all thought calculus was confusing — doing the math on the remarriage equation can get complicated quick!)

Date at least two years before considering marriage. Sound unrealistic? Think about it. The first seven months to a year of a relationship is considered the "honeymoon phase." Both of you are trying to put your best foot forward to ensure that your date responds well to you. In other words, you aren't being yourself. How many people have married during that period — and then contributed to that 75 percent divorce rate for second marriages? Christian psychiatrist and author Ross Campbell has recommended relationships of at least two-and-a-half years before marriage; people can often hide their true nature for about two years — but eventually the truth will come out. If you can keep a relationship alive and growing for two years or more, you'll have a much greater chance of choosing a suitable life mate. You have no reason to hurry. Take your time. Make absolutely sure that God is putting the relationship together. The last thing you would ever want is another failed marriage for yourself or your children.

Additional Resources

The Single Dad's Survival Guide by Mike Klumpp

My Single Mom Life by Angela Thomas

Boundaries in Dating by Henry Cloud and John Townsend

CHAPTER 19

Remarriage

Kids don't adjust and
just get over their parents' divorce —
even after 13 years.
It's a lifelong adjustment...
RON DEAL, founder of Smart Stepfamilies

Be a constructive ambassador with the other home
LAURA PETHERBRIDGE, *The Smart Stepmom*

This isn't a book on remarriage. It isn't a book on establishing a blended family.

This is a book on co-parenting. Remarriage and stepfamily issues figure in only because they will have a definite and powerful impact on your children and on your relationship with your ex-spouse—and because, when you marry again, or your ex does, there'll be one more partner in the co-parenting equation: a stepparent.

I explain this because I want to make it clear that I'm not offering a primer here on remarriage or stepfamily issues. That's much too complex an issue to deal with in one chapter, and when the time comes, I hope you'll refer to some of the excellent resources I recommend in this chapter and in the appendix, as well as others you'll find on your own. In this chapter, I'm going to address only those aspects of remarriage that affect the kids or the co-parenting TEAMM.

Even though we're limiting this discussion in that way, it's still amazingly complex. Consider:

Some of you may someday consider marrying a person without children. Perhaps he or she has been married before, and perhaps not; but you will not have to consider a co-parenting relationship on that side of the family, and you will have no children to stepparent.

Some of you may consider marrying someone with children. In that case, an ex-spouse will probably be part of the picture, and that ex-spouse may have already remarried. Therefore, you'll be stepping into a new role as stepparent to your new spouse's children, a co-parent to your spouse's ex-spouse, and an extended co-parent to the ex-spouse's new spouse ... complicated!

You'll likely have a whole new cast of in-laws to relate to – confusing enough for you, since you may still have some relationships with your past in-laws, but even more so for your kids, since they now may have four sets of grandparents and four different casts of extended family.

Then there's the obvious: Your future mate will become the new stepparent to your children and will interact with your ex-spouse.

Confused yet? It sounds like a soap opera! I list all these relationships simply to remind us that, while remarriage may be wonderful, it always is complicated – and everyone in the family is impacted by many new relationships, not least of all your kids. Intentionally managing these relationships will benefit the children – and it will also, definitely, contribute to peace of mind for you and your new spouse.

Preparing for Remarriage

Pre-engagement classes

Yep, that's right: *pre*-engagement classes. My recommendation is not that, first, you get engaged and then take pre-marital classes, but rather that first you take pre-engagement classes or counseling – *before* you get engaged. Understand what you're getting into before you get into it. The divorce rate is *so* high for second marriages that you would be wise to do everything you can to prepare yourself and your intended to not add to that sad statistic. The counseling resource "Prepare/Enrich" is an excellent series, only eight classes long. Attending these eight sessions *before* getting engaged is an ideal way to process the idea of remarriage. Waiting to do it one month before the wedding is a bad plan, since most people will decide to ignore red flags once the invitations have been sent and the dress is bought. Better to prepare first and possibly avoid more pain later.

> **Stepfamilies are like slow cookers, not microwaves.**
> RON DEAL, SMART STEPFAMILIES

Sometimes couples have found, after taking Prepare, that they need to take a little more time to learn and grow in the relationship before saying "I do." Others have found the Prepare classes to be completely affirming that they're ready to get married. Be wise: do the work before getting engaged – it will be a blessing to you, your future spouse, your children, and your future grandchildren. (See www.Prepare-Enrich.com for class locations in your area.)

Learn how to build a successful stepfamily

Ron Deal, founder of Smart Stepfamilies, is my hero on this topic. He has devoted his entire professional life to counseling stepfamilies. You can find great information and resources at his website (www.SmartStepfamilies.com), or, even better, see him live at a conference in your city. Attending a conference of his before you remarry would be a great investment in your new family. Ron has written several helpful books that explore remarriage and the dynamics of stepfamilies. I would recommend, at an absolute minimum, that together you and your intended read *The Smart Stepfamily* (Bethany House, 2002) or watch the DVD.

One of the things I enjoy most about Ron's presentation is his microwave versus crockpot analogy. We have become such a microwave, quick-reply, immediate-gratification society that we forget that blending a stepfamily or building a relationship with a new stepchild takes time – lots and lots of time. No *instant connection* button exists, no *press here for immediate trust and relationship* knob. It would certainly be easier if it worked that way; but kids take a long

time to warm up to a new stepparent, and one of the greatest gifts
you can give them while they do so is time and patience. Stepfamilies take an average of seven years to blend – so no one gets instant
gratification in this game.

Introducing your future spouse to your ex-spouse

By the time you're considering remarriage, your co-parent will
have already known about this new person, and will have probably heard many details from your children. Even if you've already
introduced your new love interest to your ex, as I suggested in the
previous chapter, it's a good idea to invite your ex to meet you and
your future spouse for dinner or coffee, to let the two of them get
to know each other a little before you're all sitting at soccer games
or ballet recitals together.

If that's totally out of the question – and for many readers it will
be, because of the difficulties in their relationship (or lack of one)
with their ex – then at least make an effort to tell your co-parent
about the person you're about to marry. Your new spouse will be a
stepparent to your ex's children. Your ex may have some anxiety
that he or she is being replaced as a parent. It's your job to initiate
the awkward conversations and help build that bridge so your children won't feel extra stress when both birth parent and stepparent
are present – as they often will be at school events and major life
events. Remember the priority: the children. Do everything possible to protect them from stressful encounters when all the parents
are present.

Allow your co-parent to ask questions of or about your intended,
and don't get defensive. We all have concerns about who is going
to be around our children, and your co-parent will have his or her
own questions and concerns – just as you would if the tables were
turned, as someday, in all likelihood, they will be. Don't let that
start a war between you. Talk calmly, sharing whatever information you feel is appropriate for your co-parent to know. And keep
in mind that the conversation is for information exchange only

—you're not asking your ex's permission or advice. You're informing your co-parent about the new person who will be in a parental
role with your shared children.

Learning to Be a Stepparent

If you're about to get married, and your soon-to-be-new-spouse also
has children, then undoubtedly you've been thinking about your
relationship with those children and your new role as their stepparent for some time. Some of you are getting along well in building
a relationship with the new kids in your life, and others are struggling. Everyone in this equation will have a significant transition
to go through—and everyone will need to extend extra grace and
patience to the others.

Here are some tips that may make things easier all around.

Even though the adults have all moved on and are starting new
lives, the kids are the ones with the hardest job. They come and go
between two completely different homes, two bedrooms, different
rules and expectations, different family dynamics—and through all
of this, they are often still hurting inside and confused about their
parents' divorce. They may truly like you, the stepparent. They
may be happy that you're in their life. But the stepparent/stepchild
relationship takes time to establish itself, from the inside out. Your
stepkids may equate liking you with disloyalty toward their birth
parent—especially if their other parent is being negative about you.
That can become a downward spiral with no easy answer.

Don't ever make the kids feel any pressure from you about what
they should call you. Labels are just that—labels. Be the one to initiate the conversation with something like, "I wanted to talk about
what we are going to call each other. I know it can be awkward
when we introduce each other at school functions or when we are
at ball games, and I don't want you to be uncomfortable with what
to say. You can call me whatever you like—what is most important
to me is that you feel relaxed and there is no pressure about anything specific. Can we brainstorm a bit and see what we can come

up with?" Don't get defensive or get your feelings hurt if they just call you by your first name. It might take years for them to move beyond that, if ever; so just be confident in the journey and don't force anything on them.

I would also encourage you to have the conversation about how they want you to introduce them. It can go something like, "I also want to ask you what will make you most comfortable when I introduce you. I can say you are my stepchild or I can say you are _____'s son/daughter (your spouse's name). Do you have any preferences I should know about or other ideas that you would prefer?" Also, let the kids know that whatever you come up with now can always be changed. If they decide in a couple months, or a couple years, that they would rather use another label, tell them that the door is always open to talk about these ideas.

One more "awkward conversation" to go ahead and talk about is, "I am not here to replace your other parent. I know your (mom/dad) really loves you and I respect that, and I don't ever want you to think I am here to try and replace him/her. I want to be another person in your life to love you and cheer for you! You are important to me and I just want you to know I am here, and that if things feel awkward or you ever want to talk about all of this, I will be happy to talk. I know when we are all at your ball games and school activities it might seem weird, but I want you to know I am going to be here for you, but never to get in the way with your real mom/dad." Saying these words out loud and clearly is very important because kids will think up things and assume things that are not true. It is critical to be the one who initiates all the uncomfortable conversations and lovingly clarifies what your intentions are. They will have no way of knowing what you think inside unless you speak up and tell them.

Remember also, don't be offended or take anything personal when you're "in the moment" of it all—like, when your stepchild runs up to their biological parents first and hugs them and high fives them and then gets caught up with teammates and maybe doesn't even acknowledge you are standing there. Don't take it personal. Don't let your emotions get in the way. Be the mature one who stands strong, lovingly, and patiently. Kids are going to forget to say "Thank you" and "I appreciate you being here" and "You matter to me" because they are kids. I have been guilty myself of assuming the worst (in the moment) and then later realizing that I was over reacting and underestimating the true loving bond I have with my husband's children.

Let the children lead the way on physical affection. Don't pressure them to hug you or sit on your lap or accept your kiss on the cheek. Let the relationship develop naturally over time. Do all you can to pour love and kindness into the kids. If the kids are comfortable with physical affection, include that as part of it; but never force it. Follow their lead.

All stepfamilies (from a child's perspective) are created out of *loss*. You're excited about your new beginning, the idea of a new blended family – but all your stepchild may be thinking of, still, is the loss of a parent to divorce or death. Your place in their family was created by the loss of someone they loved. Show great patience toward your new stepchildren; chances are, they are still sorting through their own hurt and sadness about their biological parents. Is this true in every case? No. Some kids don't even remember their other parent. In that case, you may be the long-awaited hero. But remain sensitive to your stepchildren's sense of loss.

Don't be jealous of the continued interaction between your new spouse and his or her ex, the children's other parent. The nature of co-parenting is that the co-parent will be a fixture in your life, and your spouse's, for the long haul. That should be no threat to you. Your spouse is choosing you. Whatever the past, whatever the details of his or her former relationship, your new spouse is choosing *you*! Enjoy that, and don't let yourself get caught in the mind game of being jealous just because your new spouse still has to communicate with the co-parent. If you have the ring on your finger, be confident in that. Don't waste time worrying about the memories your spouse and his or her kids' other parent may share – concentrate on your purpose in the co-parenting equation, which is not to undo the past but to build a loving and positive future. Keep your eyes and heart forward-focused, so that you can bring your very best self to the marriage – and especially to the children.

If the other parent is not yet remarried, he or she has to show up to all the ballgames and piano recitals alone, feeling like a third wheel on a bicycle. Offer to take a picture of your stepkids with their other parent. Wouldn't you appreciate that kindness, if you were in his or her shoes? You don't have to become best friends; you don't have to hang out with the other parent. Just be human. Just remember that everyone feels awkward at those events. Just remember that it's not about you – it's always about the kids!

The Power of a Positive Word

The only part of the stepparenting equation you can control is your words and your attitude. Earlier in the book, I challenged the biological co-parents to choose three positive characteristics about their former spouse to say out loud and often to their children. This helps the children see the positive identity they have with their other parent, and it improves their self-esteem.

Now I want you, the prospective stepparent, to do the very same thing. New stepmoms, pick three positive comments you can make to your stepchildren about their mom. New stepdads, pick three positive comments you can make to your stepchildren about their dad. I know it sounds crazy; but if you want to build a strong relationship with your future stepkids, you'll do this – for them!

Don't skip this. This isn't optional. This is important.

1. _____

2. _____

3. _____

Now I want you to say those things to the children the next time you see them – today if possible. Don't wait for an easy or convenient time – that time will never come. Just do it. Then do it again in a few days.

Take every opportunity to remind your stepkids that you are not replacing their biological parent; you are an additional person who loves them, one more person in their corner. Tell them you realize they will always love their mom or dad, and that you don't want to change or interfere with that love. Tell them (out loud!): "It's okay for you to love all of us. It's not a game of favorites. You don't have to choose." Acknowledge to the kids that sometimes it might feel awkward to have all their parents and stepparents in the same room, such as at school events. Tell them to just relax and not worry about that.

These words will plant seeds that will eventually blossom – and it will be beautiful! It might take seven years to harvest, but it's worth the wait.

Resources

I'm so thankful for extended resources on this topic – they can truly transform the process from frustrating and painful to fruitful and enjoyable.

For those becoming a stepmom, Ron Deal's newest release with co-author Laura Petherbridge is a must-read for you. *The Smart Stepmom*[19] is an honest look at the process and will bring laughter and understanding to any new stepmom. I know, because as I have been on that journey I have referred to it several times for advice and ideas from people who have been down the path ahead of me. You can find the book on Ron Deal's website (mentioned earlier) or Laura Petherbridge's site: www .LauraPetherbridge.com. Be careful where you read this book – it will make you laugh out loud sometimes. You'll find yourself saying, "Really? You went

> Trust in the Lord with all your heart
> and lean not on your own understanding.
> Acknowledge Him in all your ways and He will make straight your paths.
> PROVERBS 3:5-6

through that, too?" I have embarrassed myself a few times at the coffee shop while reading this one; it reads like a good conversation with friends. I know you'll enjoy it.

For dads, I recommend *The Smart Stepdad*,[20] also by Ron Deal. The book offers advice for men on how to connect with stepchildren, be a godly role model, and keep the bond strong with your spouse. Ron also gives perspective on what the kids are going through and how to handle discipline, dealing with your wife's ex, and even ideas on hugging your stepchildren. A must-read for all stepdads!

You have an awesome opportunity — to be a role model and a positive influence in the lives of your stepchildren. Be an example they can be proud to follow. Walk well in their presence, and let your life speak louder than your words. Be a solution seeker and a loving, stable part of the family.

PART SEVEN

And Into the Future …

Co-Parenting for Life — Even After Child Support Ends

Who will walk me down the aisle;
who will give me away?
MARCELLA, an adult child of divorce
who is engaged to be married

My parents divorced,
but they never missed important events in my life,
including the night *my* first son was born!
MIKE, age 47

From the earliest pages of this book, we've been talking about a co-parenting TEAMM. By now you know exactly what it means: The End Adult Matters Most—the "end adult" being your own children when they reach adulthood. And what we're talking about in this chapter is just that—the payoff. The goal you've been working for not just throughout this book but throughout the years of parenting your kids—through elementary school, middle school, high school, and college. Through the years of tough negotiations with your co-parent, of maybe also incorporating two new stepparents into the mix. Working through tough decisions on who pays for the braces, who picks up what portion of the college tuition, who buys the computer.

Close your eyes and peer twenty years into the future. What age will your children be? Can you imagine what they will look like as adults? What kind of car will they drive? What kind of job will they have? What will their future spouses look like? How many kids will they have?

What milestones will they have accomplished along the way?

Twenty birthdays will have come and gone, along with junior-high band concerts and proms and science fairs. They will see yearbooks, high-school graduation, the first day of college, and moving into a new dorm room. They will have college experiences and another graduation. They will get their first real job and their first real paycheck (finally!). They will have dating experiences sprinkled along the path—and maybe will already be married twenty years from now. That means you'll have already been through the planning, the dress, the tux, the rehearsal dinner, the wedding day, and the reception. Whew—my head is already spinning! How about yours?

My point is: As our kids grow up and create their adult lives, who are the two people who want to be on the front row of that experience—watching, encouraging, directing, listening, celebrating, and cheering them forward? For most kids, both parents will always want to be there—Mom and Dad. Always. Other people might join you on that front row of life, but you will always want to know and to experience these milestones with your children. Your love for your kids will become a stable, strong launching pad for them to springboard from, but even when they're grown it will never end. And if your co-parent has been involved with you through the long years of raising those kids, then long after the last child support check is exchanged, your lives will still be overlapping.

Having grown up between two homes and two divorced (and remarried) parents, the one thing I can say that is still true today—more than forty years after their divorce—is that they both still love me deeply. They both wanted to participate in all of the many milestones along the way. They both wanted to be there on graduation day and moving me into college. They both wanted to see their little granddaughter, Angelia, when she was first born. Their lives still intersect; they have not exchanged a child support check in over two decades, but their lives still intersect on occasion. One of my parents lives in Tennessee and the other in Colorado. But for most of my post-high-school life, they lived in the same state, about two hours apart. And on holidays and trips home from college, I still felt torn between the two—like I never had enough time to see them both and to make them both feel like I had been "fair and equal" with my time.

I've heard similar laments from many other adult children of divorce. One of the most common frustrations I hear is that their parents always made everything about "them"—about the parents. Even grown up with children of their own, children of divorce still feel that continual pull between their parents. Graduation days and wedding days are too often not about the kids—they end up being about all the parents' unresolved issues. If I had a dollar for every agonizing story I have heard from college kids and young adults (especially those who got married with divorced parents present), I would be a rich, retired woman. When co-parents make it all about themselves, they may be damaging their kids for life.

Recently I talked with Anna, a woman in her early twenties, who was planning her wedding day. When the topic of how divorce impacts kids came up, she had so much bottled-up frustration to express it took an hour for her to share it with me. She said it took forever to even find a way to script the wedding invitation, let alone all the drama she was experiencing between her mom and dad. They both wanted to be involved and both wanted to help her pay for the wedding—so far so good. But it became a third world war over who was going to get all the attention and the spotlight, who was going to get the credit, who was going to do what. Anna told me she had so many tear-filled nights that she just wanted to call the whole thing off! She's deeply in love with her fiancé, but the continual conflict and drama between her divorced parents was absolutely wearing her out. She and her fiancé had truly considered eloping.

She finally said to her mother, "This is not your wedding; this is *my* wedding. This is not about your divorce from dad; this is about *my* new marriage. This is not about getting the spotlight on you; it's supposed to be about celebrating *my* new chapter of life."

She had spent so much energy for so many years babysitting her parents' emotions that she couldn't do it anymore.

What about you? It's easy for us to sit here and think, *Oh, I won't be like that.* But trust me—when it comes down to who sits on the front pew and who sits on the second pew, who walks the bride down the aisle and who gets to give her away—those conflicts can bring out the most ugly and territorial sides of a divorced parent. Then you throw in the stepparents, step or half siblings, and the next thing you have is a Jerry Springer war—either all at once or piece by piece through your children.

I went to a wedding recently that broke my heart. The bride, Erin, was from a divorced family. Her father had remarried when she was about five years old and had chosen to live very near his ex-wife so that he could participate intensely in his daughter's life. He was at every piano recital, every school event, every church event. Most years, he drove her ten hours across the country on Christmas Eve so that she could have half of Christmas with her mom's extended family and half with her dad. He had sacrificed and gone way beyond any child-support requirement or parenting plan decree.

They had raised Erin by splitting parenting time in half. They had worked well together all those years, and Erin's father had proven to be a wonderful father, more attentive and involved than many traditional fathers. He invested in his little girl and loved her well.

But weddings have a way of bringing up old hurts. Erin's mother apparently saw this as a great opportunity to get back at Erin's dad for how much she had been hurt by him nineteen years earlier. Erin did not walk down the aisle with her dad; worse, the way they chose to inform her dad was through the wedding coordinator, who handed him a piece of paper at the rehearsal that said "Escorting bride down the aisle—Joe Smith." Who was Joe Smith? Joe was the mother's boyfriend—not her husband, not Erin's stepfather—just the mom's boyfriend. Erin's mom took away the thing every dad looks forward to—his little girl's wedding day, and the few (but significant) steps they walk together, down an aisle, as she symbolically transforms from little girl to woman.

Nineteen years of pent-up frustration and hurt came out on a white printed piece of paper in six little words.

Erin's dad had been given no warning. I was stunned. The tears I saw well up in Erin's dad's eyes will never leave my memory. He looked as if he had just been punched in the gut. All the years he had invested in Erin, all the sacrifices, the thousands of miles of driving through the middle of the night to pick up his daughter and to drop her off, it was as if none of it mattered.

I have no idea how Erin and her mom negotiated this behind the scenes, or what Erin truly wanted on her wedding day; but from the outside looking in, I saw it as an exact example of what *not* to do when planning a wedding between divorced parents.

Even if Erin had wanted Joe to be her escort, even if Joe had been her stepdad for ten years (none of which was true), they still should have taken into account the soul of a father who truly loves his daughter and had proven to be a faithful father for over nineteen years post-divorce. And this one act rippled beyond the father; his family—his brothers and sisters and his parents (Erin's grandparents)—got the message that they were unimportant, that this event was only all about the mom. As the wedding day unfolded, that theme continued to be true. The slide show that ran during the dinner included thirty or forty shots of Erin and her mom and only one of her father. The seating arrangements pushed Erin's dad and his extended family to the outskirts. The photographer was directed in curt tones to get just get a few pictures of "that side of the family."

> We make a living by what we get; we make a life by what we give.
> SIR WINSTON CHURCHILL

What a true injustice—and what a horrible way to get even. Erin's dad had proven himself to be a patient and loving man, but I am sure he will never forget the hurt of that day.

I can almost see you shaking your head, thinking now (when your kids are young) that you would never do something like

Erin's mom did. Oh, how I pray you won't! How I pray that your children will all grow up with the opportunity to come and go *freely* between you and your former spouse, to not feel guilty for loving you both. I pray that when you move your kids into the college dorm, it will be done with true joy and true peace—or that if you can't manage true joy and peace, that you'll at least reign in your own emotions so your children can make it a positive experience. I want to see your kids smile on the day they get married—not just on the outside, for the photographer, but truly smile *inside* because they have two amazing co-parents who have walked well together.

Two co-parents who realize that none of this is about them ...

It's all about the kids!

CHAPTER 21

What Will Your Kids Remember?

My parents were divorced,
but they always got along.
CHARLEY, age 49

It seemed like my dad abandoned our family.
I always thought he was mad at us,
but I guess my mom was really mad at him
and she told him to stay away—
how could a mother be so heartless?
DANIELLE, age 32

I never felt torn between my parents.
I always felt like I had extra people to love me—
Stepparents, stepgrandparents—
all of them were wonderful!
ALEC, age 37

My dad was amazing.
He was the rock that held us all together.
My mom was a roller coaster,
but my dad was the rock!
MIA, age 23

In chapter 20, I had you fast-forward twenty years. Let's go back to that same place in time—twenty years into the future. Ask yourself: What will your kids say about how you co-parented them? What will be their greatest memories? Soccer games and birthday parties where everyone got along peacefully and a good time was had by all? Or will it be 7–11 parking lots and Christmas Eves

with police lights flashing, when your kids sat terrified and humili-
ated, tears streaming down their faces?

What will *your* children look back on and remember about
you? What will they remember about having two homes? What
will they remember about homework and graduation days? Shopping for school clothes, family holiday traditions, the interaction
between Mom and Dad?

You have the power to give your children a happy and fulfill-
ing childhood. Even if your children's other parent turns out to
be either a nonparticipant or a monster, you can still do all you
can – which is a lot – to make your children's story one of joy and
smiles, peace and togetherness, even though you are raising them
between separate households. Part of that power rests in the loving
and thoughtful and constructive and wise things you choose to do.
And part of it will rest in your decision and ability to suck it up and
just keep it shut, knowing that your words bring either life or death
to the soul of your children.

The choices you make will be reflected in the very fiber of your
children's being. If you choose anger and hate, resentfulness and
unforgiveness – your children will reap destruction. If you choose
peace and forgiveness, optimism and forward thinking, your children will have a far greater likelihood of enjoying their life. This
isn't rocket science or brain surgery – it's grown-up, mature, intentional living. It doesn't happen because you wing it. It happens
when you intentionally create it.

I interview adult children of divorce at my seminars and events.
The vast differences between the ways they were brought up amaze
me. Some talk of shared Christmas holidays with both divorced
parents. Some have even recalled taking a trip with their parents
and stepparents all on the same cruise. Wow! I admit that's probably unrealistic for most; but even those who have much quieter
and more conventional happy memories relate them to me with
shining eyes and smiles.

On the other hand, some talk of noncustodial parents who
abandoned ship completely after a few years of getting nothing

but anger and frustration from the custodial parent—and the holes those missing parents left in the hearts of their children are enormous. Many of those adult children of divorce have spent their whole lives trying to fill that hole in unhealthy ways, being wounded time and time again simply because their custodial parent could not let go of the past and their noncustodial parent gave up.

Others of these young adults simmer with anger because one parent used them as a spy and a weapon throughout their childhood—and now they won't even speak to that parent. I have heard stories of abuse that was ignored, swept under the carpet, because a parent was too focused on his or her own distractions—dating? career?—to notice what was happening.

The pendulum swings wide between stories of hope and stories of hate.

What stories will your children recall? If I interview them in twenty years at one of my events and ask how well their divorced parents co-parented, or whether they grew up listening to one parent badmouth the other, or which parent they respect most and feel safest with because of the way each handled co-parenting, or whether they always felt free to love both parents—what will they say?

> In all these things we are more than conquerors through him who loved us. For I am convinced that neither death nor life, neither angels nor demons, neither the present nor the future, nor any powers, neither height nor depth, nor anything else in all creation, will be able to separate us from the love of God that is in Christ Jesus our Lord.
>
> ROMANS 8:37—39

What if I asked your children those questions right now? What would they tell me about the way their lives are going today? What would they tell me about you? Do you smile when they leave to visit their other parent and wish them a good visit—or do you give them a guilt trip about leaving? Do they feel like you are stable and happy, the grown up, the one in control—or do they feel like they have to take care of you and be responsible for your sadness? Do they feel free to be a kid and do the things kids do at their specific age – or do they have to play the role of the grown up and run the household because you're out partying, running away from the pain and the stress?

What about the words they hear you say about their other parent? Would they recount to me positive and life-filled words, or would they repeat words of anger, negativity, and hate?

How do you think your kids feel about the role of money in your family? Are your kids the go-between who calls the other parent about child support and money needed for summer camp, or do they know that the money issue is being taken care of between their parents, so that the kids can simply say, "That's not my job; I let my parents work that out."

Time for another exercise – the last one in this book. I want you to rate yourself on your current performance as a co-parent, on a scale of 1 – 10, with the "1" indicating a poor performance that creates stress or sadness for your kids and the "10" a great one – meaning that your kids are free of your baggage and enjoying their life between the two parents they love. Here's the catch: I don't want you to rate yourself on how well *you* think you're doing; I want you to rate yourself on how you think your *kids* would say you are doing – right now, today.

Here's the list. Date it, and rate yourself from 1 to 10 in each of the indicated areas:

Indicators of Healthy Co-Parenting

Date today: _____

_____ We give our children the freedom to love both of their parents.

_____ The transition between our homes is smooth and positive.

_____ We discuss and deal with financial matters in a rational way.

_____ We work to minimize the stress of Christmas and other holidays.

_____We encourage our children to love and maintain ties with both extended families.

_____We enjoy being at our children's functions and are there to enhance our children's happiness.

_____We recognize the developmental stages of our children and let them enjoy their childhood.

_____We take care of responsibilities as adults and do not put pressure on the children to do our job.

_____We encourage our children to have photos of their other parent in their bedroom.

_____We tell our children it is okay to talk about how much they miss the other parent.

_____We speak highly of the other parent to our children, with at least three specific compliments.

_____We prioritize our time with the children and are fully engaged with them and focused on them.

_____We communicate regularly with our co-parent at pre-designated meetings or conference calls.

_____We do not allow or utilize the children as messengers or "go-betweens" on anything.

_____We incorporate other friends and activities into our lives to enhance our self care and happiness.

_____We are working with our co-parent and stepparents to raise healthy and well-adjusted children.

When you finish, review the list and commit to doing better in the areas where you think your kids are struggling most. In fact, write down a plan for yourself for what you'll do to improve in those areas.

And you *can* improve. Believe me—I'm constantly finding new ways to coordinate life with my daughter's dad that make things happier and better for our daughter, and you will too. My greatest hope is that your children will look back and smile, twenty years from today, knowing that they have two parents who love them unconditionally, and that it's okay that they love them both.

Your co-parenting decisions every day will design the fabric of your child's story. May their colors be vibrant, may their history be strong, and may their hearts be free.

The book is nearly over—but this is *only the beginning* of your child's story. Write it well, my dear friend. I'm giving you a standing ovation right now because you are reading these words, near the very end of this book, meaning that you have already shown a willingness to invest yourself on behalf of your children. Getting a copy of this book, taking the time to read it (probably late at night) in a life that is no doubt filled to an uncomfortable overflow with the tasks of raising children and making a living reveals that you are running this race well. Your children will benefit if you implement even one idea from this book. Because of that, I believe that your children will *not* be simply a statistic of the divorce wars—and that *you,* as a co-parent, are going to defy all the norms.

And now, as a sign of accomplishment that you've finished the tough task of grappling through this book, with all of the difficult issues we've tackled, and as a token of your commitment to your kids, please sign the co-parenting agreement you'll find after the Conclusion. It may seem silly to some of you, but just think—you're putting your signature to a commitment that involves your kids, and that's not something to be taken lightly. This way, when the going gets tough in co-parenting and you just want to quit, you'll remember—you signed a commitment.

Do your kids a favor: Promise me that you'll re-read this book once a year. Here's why: The circumstances and challenges you face in co-parenting will change every year as your children grow, and because of that

> When my spirit grows faint within me, it is You who know my way.
> PSALM 142:3

you will, most likely, pick up on something new each time you read this. For me, reading is like watching a good movie—I always catch more details the second and third times through than I did the first. It will be that way next time you read this book.

Here's another encouragement: Please find a friend who will be a co-parenting "sounding board" and a consistent accountability partner in your life. Look for someone a few years ahead of you in the co-parenting journey and ask if you can keep the door open to talk and brainstorm about your family's circumstances. Don't choose someone who will just get angry at your ex and make the situations worse, and don't choose someone stuck in their own resentment of the past. Find someone level-headed and mature who will affirm and support your goal of growing into a stable and cooperative co-parent who makes healthy choices for yourself and your children. Loan this book to the person you choose – and after they've read it, you can discuss it to spur your joint creativity.

And when you've come up with those creative ideas that enhance cooperative co-parenting, please email me and share them so that I can learn from *your* experiences. We are all learning and growing everyday in how to walk well as co-parents, and you can help my journey just as I hope this book has helped yours. Check in anytime at our website for free article downloads, co-parent "coaching" tips, and other co-parenting stories and resources: www.CoparentingInternational.com.

I'm here with you, backpack and all, taking one small step forward every day. I'll keep my eyes out for you along the way, hoping to see you in the shady resting places and hear the details of your day. May peace and hope reign in your heart, today and forever. May God redeem every part of your story and of the legacy you are protecting as you raise your children well!

A companion in the
co-parenting journey,
Tammy

Be Brave!

What Great Co-Parenting Can Do

Here's a testimony to what great co-parenting has the potential to produce for *your* children. The words you choose to say and to leave unsaid can produce a beautiful harvest for millions to enjoy.

Many of you, no doubt, have heard of Dr. John Trent. A leading author and national speaker on marriage and family who has been married for thirty-two years, he conducts "Strong Families in Stressful Times" seminars in churches across America. In the past seven years alone, Dr. Trent has spoken to over 100,000 people in more than sixty-five major cities. He has also spoken to over 750,000 men at Promise Keepers conferences in stadium events across the United States. Dr. Trent has also served two churches as their family pastor and has been a featured guest on radio and television programs like *The Oprah Winfrey Show*, *AM Northwest*, San Diego's *Morning Spotlight*, Cleveland's *Morning Exchange*, Dallas's *Good Morning, Texas!*, Focus on the Family's radio broadcast, Dr. Charles Swindoll's *Insight for Living*, the Billy Graham Evangelistic Association crusade broadcasts, *The 700 Club*, and many, many more.

Dr. Trent has authored and co-authored more than a dozen award-winning and bestselling books, including the million-selling book *The Blessing*. As of 2004, more than 2,300,000 copies of his adult and children's books are in print, in nine different languages.

Clearly, Dr. Trent has accomplished more in his lifetime than most of us can even imagine doing. But here's what is even more amazing: Dr. Trent's parents divorced when he was very young. That's right—John Trent is one of those children of divorce whose future we worry about. Yet look at what God has done with his life! He is evidence that parents can raise kids to defy every statistic about children of divorce.

In his recent book *Breaking the Cycle of Divorce*, Dr. Trent shares two simple things he believes contributed to his ability to break the repetitive cycle of divorce:

1. His mother never spoke ill of his dad.

2. His mother always spoke to John about God's intention for lifelong marriage.[21]

If we were in a Southern Baptist church right now, I'd be shouting "Amen!" Notice how John's mother was wise in what she said —and in what she didn't say. She held back from saying anything negative about his father. *And* she spoke words of encouragement to him about God's true intention for lifelong marriage.

Our words matter. The words that you've spoken in the past few days to your children—or that they overheard you saying—are at work right now forming your children's destiny. Our words and actions are at work *right now* shaping our children's future marriages and parenting skills.

Let's make sure they're as constructive and as wise as the words of John Trent's mother. If we do, maybe our own children will be able to face life with the confidence and desire to make a difference that John Trent has.

Be Brave

Alice has three children. She's passionate about being a great co-parent. She has come to several of our seminars; she has read every article I've written, and we have talked for hours in church parking lots about her specific situation and all the complications that come with the co-parenting journey. I know she wants to be the best parent on the planet. I know she wants to walk well in front of her children.

I know all of that, and so does she. But that doesn't mean she always feels capable of it. Sometimes she feels like she can't take one more step. Sometimes she believes the lie that her kids might be better off without her. Thank God, she has never acted on those depressing thoughts or said those hurt-filled words to her children.

Alice is often discouraged because, like many of you, her divorce was difficult. She has also faced breast cancer, chemotherapy, and extensive surgeries. She lost all of her hair—twice. Yet, somehow, she is still moving forward.

I tell Alice's story to illustrate that each of us has a million unique details to our circumstances. Some of our battles are truly more enormous than any human should ever have to face … and yet there they are, day after day.

I also know this: Every day is a new beginning. Every morning cup of coffee is a chance to breathe deep, prepare myself, and then get up and do the day differently, better, than the one before. Every long hot shower is a time to regroup and start over. I can't ever go back and undo what has been done. For those of us who've been through a divorce—where would we even start? The list of things that need a do-over is too long.

What we can do is walk boldly into today and decide to just be brave.

What power those two words have: Be brave. They have gotten me through so many dark moments. They've been a motto in my life since my dear friend, single dad Levi, spoke them back to me at a time when I was weak and scared. He reminded me of who I am and what I am made of. He reminded me that I am never truly alone in this world, and that God loves me more than my human mind can ever comprehend. "Tammy," he said, "just go in there and be brave!"

So I say to you, dear companions on this journey of winding roads and hurting hearts, we must be brave! When we fall down we must get back up. When we say the wrong thing, we must own it and apologize. When we act in anger toward our co-parent, we must call them the next day and acknowledge that we were wrong. When we act selfishly and the kids are hurt by it, we must clear the air and make it up to them. When the long, lonely nights stretch on forever after divorce, we must suck it up and remind ourselves that this is just one phase of our life, and that it's only temporary — that it gets better.

When life is just too hard and too much is required of you — be brave.

When your ex-spouse marries the person he or she left you for, making them your kids' stepparent — for the sake of your kids, be brave.

When you are at your child's school event or at church, sitting alone in what seems like an auditorium full of married parents, be brave.

When there's too much month at the end of the money — be brave.

When no one else seems willing to take responsibility, along with you, for the welfare of your kids, leaving you to shoulder the whole burden — be brave.

After all — bravery is a completely appropriate response for a child of the King.

> *I will praise you, O Lord, with all my heart ...*
> *When I called, you answered me;*
> *You made me bold and stouthearted.*
> PSALM 138: 1, 3

My Co-Parenting Promise

Today I commit myself to be a cooperative co-parent with:

_____

For the sake of my children, I will make every effort to be intentional, flexible, thoughtful, forgiving, kind, and merciful. I will do whatever it takes to parent forward, guiding my children toward whole and healthy living, to minimize the divided self, and to enhance my children's experience of living with *one heart* in *two homes*.

In honor of (names of children): _____

_____

Date: _____

Signed: _____

Acknowledgments

Pappa God: I could never have imagined what a beautiful life story you had in mind when you began my journey. I am overwhelmed with all you have blessed me with and how you have given beauty for ashes and brought Redemption to all my brokenness. I will continue to say thank you with every day of my life as I seek to glorify you and bring HOPE to hurting places all around the world.

There are so many who have been significant along the way, and it would take a whole novel to express my heart of gratitude to each of you individually, yet you each hold a unique chapter in my life story ...

From all the years *before* the book: Steve and Cora Alley; Erica, Jean, and Gary Ehman; Carolyn and the Zellitti family; Kirsten Fletcher; Kelly, Chip, Wanda, and Troy Lindsey; Melody Joy Griffith; Kathy "Ori" Smith; Jen N. and the Nichols family; Leslie and David Fullmer; Jill Foster; Kathie Tycksen; Tammie and Brian Lees; Ramona Hunter-Turmezei; Ruthie Johnson; Bruce Koblish; Judy and Phil Claiborne; Steve and Kim Hayes (Steve, you planted the seed for this book when you gave me hope in my own crisis!); Jerry and Fern Sutton; Jerry and Barbara Highfill; Rachel and Mike Cole; Michelle and David Amster; Lucy and Fred Kurtz; Maria and Greg Yova; Betty Bennett and all the Bennett family (I will always love you, and I am so thankful for the way Angelia's life is such a beautiful reflection of each of you! Thanks for the "Tammy Lipstick" memories too!).

For those who have supported the vision of Co-Parenting International with your time, donations, creativity, and your hearts: Neal and Wendy Joseph; Jana and Kevin Jackson; Bill and Jessie

Van De Griek; Everton and Eboni Heron; Larry "Coach Mo" Moshell; Debby and Paul Monaghan; DeeAnne and Keith Bogle; Cricket Sehr; Steve Gilreath; Chaz Corzine; Holly Whaley; Theresa Johnson; David and Joy Smallwood; Derek Anderson; Troy and Heather Drulman; Scott Hines; Dewey Cowan; Martha and Malcolm Greenwood; Jeff and Laura Helton; Jeff Schulte; Lloyd Shadarach; Denise Peyton (I would have been lost without you!); Calvin and Nicole Delah; Kim Hill; Sharon Rhoden; Angela Thomas-Pharr; John Trent; Elisa Morgan; Ray and Robin McKelvy; Constance Rhodes; Demetrus Stewart; Jodi Skulley (and the team at Parent Life); Suellen Roberts (and Women in Christian Media); Celeste LaReau (and the TN Christian Chamber); Jan Shober; MOTIVO (and all the families!); Tony and Ingrid Rosario; TRASE; Eric and Anglie Mullett; Marcela Gomez (and the TN Hispanic Chamber); Bryan McKnight; Kim Bindel-Ford; Anadara; Shirley Logan; Kim and Bobby Sagmiller; Ken Canfield; Stephanie Smith; Flower DeRaadt; Sam Mullins (and all your monkeys!); Derek Young; Miss Patty Cake; Joe Greene; Josh Stalls; Sara De Lascurain; Steve Siler; Scott Krippayne; Tony Wood; Sue Foster; Brenda Delgado; Teresa White; Natalie Gillespie; Melinda Seibert; Michelle York; Andy Dunn; Carol Johnson; Dana Ashley; Amy and Dave Welday (my MD!); Dax Edwards; Deb (WMPL-BL!!) Hayes; Chrys and John Howard (your family is a vision to my heart!); Joneal Kirby; Donna Contestible; Brian and Heidi Petak; Christine Thomson; Alicia Lewis; Rainey Brown; Kim Osment; Jessica Robin Folkins; Joel and Terri Hill; Joey Elwood; Josh MacLeod; Rhonda (PP!) Livers; Monica Schmelter; Todd and Erin Stevens; Douglas and Creel Pittman; Jim and Kathy Anderson; Mark and Sue Funderburg; Karen Moore Artl; Charlie Dodrill; Jen Abbas de Jong; Richard Abbey; Larry and the whole Puckett family; Jennie and Michael Knight; Jennifer and Miguel Figueroa; Sarah and Mike Schatz; Charlie Redmond; Mary Grace and Rob Birkhead; Lanette Strimaitis; Chris Burnett; Byron Spradlin; Marilou and Benny Profitt; Ben Wright; Anitra and Tim Williams; Randi, Jill, and Nicholas Marin; Vicki and

Jack Mullins; Nic Eagles; Bonnie and Dick Gygi; and the whole "Locker Room" team.

Ron and Nan Deal, Smart Stepfamilies, International: Ron, you have *always* been my hero in the way you communicate and bring clarity to families. I mean it when I say, "When I grow up, I want to be just like Ron Deal!" Steve Grissom, Church Initiative / DivorceCare: Steve, your relentless commitment to bring resources to hurting people is an inspiration and I am personally grateful for how your materials helped me heal! Thank you for continuing to support the calling on my life! Martha Austin-White: YOU are the reason I went to grad school! You are the counselor I can only hope to be one day! Melissa Trevathan, Sissy Goff, Betsy Cashman, David Thomas, Jeremy Shapiro, Pat McCurdy, and all the team at Daystar Counseling: Thank you for loving children and families and bringing HOPE to so many! Nashville Area Association of Christian Counselors and the YMCA of Middle TN, along with the governing Boards of Directors: it is an honor to serve with you. Thank you for your continued support.

Thank you to all the passionate experts who have been quoted in the manuscript: acclaimed authors, researchers, counselors, national organizations, and so many real-life friends who have allowed me to share your stories.

Trevecca Nazarene University and Trevecca Community Church: Denise and Dan Boone, Nancy and Don Dunlap, Debbie and Peter Wilson, Joyce Sloan, Steve (RB!) Stride, Joy Wells, Ron Mauer, Terry Pruitt, Jan and Don Harvey, Heather Ambrefe, Susan Lahey, Jan Greathouse, Elizabeth Streight, Jay Sheffield, Rick Hill, Keli and Sam Green, Glenda and Paul Bolling, Carol Maxon, Gail and Steve Pusey, Sara and Chris Rayman, Brenda Patterson, Jayme Crowley, Paula Mate, Ruth Kinnersley, Prilla Speer, Kathy Baugher, Holly Whitby, John Ludeman, Tom Middendorf, the AMAZING "SRT" Team, Abbie VanDerPuy, Renee Carrier, Paula and Marvin Jones, Karan and Dwight Gunter, Lindsay and Jamin Wentworth, Rick Underwood, Mary Lou and Luis Del Rio, Joe and Valerie Drake, Nina and Moody Gunter,

Jack Duncan, Dr. Reed … It is an honor to do life with all of you, personally and professionally, and I am in awe of all that God has done and will continue to do as my personal Trevecca "legacy" continues to expand. To God be ALL Glory!!

Wes Yoder, the MOST AMAZING agent a girl could dream of! Thank you for the support, wisdom, and insightful contributions along the way! Dave Lambert, my editor, where have you been all my life? I look forward to many more projects together! Sandy Vander Zicht, when you walked into my life I knew I had found my publishing home and I am honored to be represented by your team at Zondervan. Thank you to all the "Z-Team" for getting behind this project, especially Tom Dean, Londa Alderink, Robin Geelhoed, Becky Philpott, Janelle Wing, Kristi Arbogast, Court-ney Lasater, Cindy Wilson, Brad Hill, Bridgette Brooks, Jackie Aldridge, Joyce Ondersma, Jeff Bowden, Rod Carpenter, and Heather Wilson. I believe generations to come will be impacted by all of us, together, sharing this message of HOPE! I pray, in heaven, God will allow each of you to see the millions of lives you have impacted by putting your hands and hearts to the publishing plow. Your work is changing hearts and impacting eternity. Thank you!!

Mi familia: Mom (Thank you for all the amazing opportunities you gave me growing up! We'll always be the "two cutest girls from Denver!"), Dad (I love you and thanks for being so active in my life. DFTW and thanks for all the "foto foto" memories!), Josie (thanks for being a great stepmom even though I never liked to dust and sweep!), John (thanks for being such a fun stepdad and cooking me crispy bacon on Saturday mornings!), Daniel (my favorite brother and an amazing uncle and teacher), Anitra (my favorite sister, educator, and an amazing mom) and all the Gallegos and Grasmick families. I am so thankful that out of the millions of families in the world, that God rooted me into the two best families in Rocky Ford! I carry forward, into my family, so many traditions and legacies that will always live on through my children because of those roots. From green chili and wedding marches to sunflowers and Rocky Ford watermelons, I love all the unique elements that represent our families!

To the Daughtry family: it is an honor to call myself a Daughtry and to enjoy being loved by you all. Thank you for welcoming me into all the family fun and traditions. I look forward to many more relaxing days on the river and many more days in our pj's (Mom D). I love you all!

Amanda Dawn dot com: You are radiant and so full of LIFE! Thank you for being so real and honest in our journey together and for letting me into your heart. I treasure you and I appreciate all the whirlwind of fun you bring to our lives. I know your mom is smiling as she watches you and listens from heaven. You are making her proud in so many ways! Keep writing and singing and sharing your gifts! In your mom's words, I echo: "Keep Lookin' Up!" I love you, Amanda!

Jenna Diane: Sweet girl, you have added deep JOY and so much laughter to my life. I have enjoyed your senior year together, and as you bravely step into your next chapter at Trevecca Nazarene University, please know I will always be here to love you and to support you. You are a beautiful reflection of your mom and you carry her name well. Enjoy college, and whatever God calls you to in the path ahead, I'll be right here cheering for you along the way! I love you, Jenna!

Jaron Shane: How amazing it has been to have a SON! You are the most creative, funny, carefree, and hilarious young man I know (and the smartest too!). I pray you never lose your sense of humor and that you always keep your heart anchored in God's Truth. Your mom is watching and giggling along with us all as you grow up, and I know she knows how much you love her. I look forward to seeing all that God does with your life – you are amazing! I love you, Jaron!

Angelia, I continue to dedicate my first calling in co-parenting to YOU and your life experience. Thank you for letting me tell our story, and I look forward to seeing how God will use YOU to speak up and be an advocate for others. I can't wait to read your future column, *"Ask Angelia!"* You have a beautiful soul and it's breathtaking to watch you as you continue to become an amazing young woman of God. You are brave and mighty, and I love you to the moon!

And to my sweet soul mate, Jay ... you are my heartbeat and my deepest joy! Every single day, every single breath is MORE AMAZING than I could have ever imagined because I get to share it all with you. You make "me" a better me! Thank you for making me laugh, for listening to all my stories and dreams, for your Godly wisdom and insight (especially on this book!), for holding my hand and my heart so tenderly in your care. You have redeemed *every* dream and every hope I had for love and family. Thank you for leading us all so well and being the strong foundation to our family. Your joy and deep love have transformed my life! I look forward to growing old with you, grandparenting with you, and our ever romantic kitchen dances ... God sure knew what he was doing when he brought us together!! Thank you for being the first smile of the morning and the last kiss of every night! I love loving you! ♥

Resources

DVDs for Divorced Parents

One Heart, Two Homes: The Voice of Co-parenting, (2009). Four hours of content by ten guest presenters (experts, counselors, pastors, adult children of divorce, and a panel of teenagers living between two homes). Available at www.CoparentingInternational.com.

One Heart, Two Homes: Small Group Resource Kit, (2011). Ten weeks of DVD content to be used in a small group discussion setting with single parents and stepparents. Can be used in school settings, church settings, or for personal small group experiences. Kit includes DVDs, workbooks, audio, and promotional materials. Available at www.CoparentingInternational.com.

The Best Interests of the Child, How to Save Our Children When We Can't Save Our Marriage, by Dr. Warren Farrell (2006). Available at www.WarrenFarrell.com.

The Smart Stepfamily (DVD) by Ron L. Deal. Eight sessions on two DVDs; Participant/Leader Study Guide. Useful for small groups, Bible classes, and personal home study. Available at www.Smart StepFamilies.com.

Books for Divorced Parents

Boundaries with Kids, by Dr. Henry Cloud and Dr. John Townsend (Zondervan, 2001).

Boundaries with Teens, by Dr. John Townsend (Zondervan, 2006).

Dads at a Distance: An Activities Handbook For Strengthening Long Distance Relationships, by the National Institute for Building Long Distance Relationships (A&E Publishing, 2001).

DivorceCare: Hope, Help and Healing During and After Your Divorce, by Steve Grissom and Kathy Leonard (Thomas Nelson, 2006).

Falling Apart in One Piece: One Optimist's Journey Through the Hell of Divorce, by Stacy Morrison (Simon & Schuster, 2010).

Helping Children Survive Divorce: What to Expect, How to Help, by Dr. Archibald D. Hart (Thomas Nelson, 1997).

Hope No Matter What: Helping Your Children Heal After Divorce, by Kim Hill and Lisa Harper (Regal, 2008).

Hugs for Single Moms: Stories, Sayings, and Scriptures to Encourage and Inspire, by Melanie Hemry (Howard Books, 2005).

In Every Pew Sits a Broken Heart, by Ruth Graham (Zondervan, 2004).

Life in the Blender: Living in a Stepfamily – A Booklet for Teens, by Ron L. Deal (Focus on the Family, 2007).

Moving Forward After Divorce: Practical Steps to Healing Your Hurts, Finding Fresh Perspective, Managing Your New Life, by David and Lisa Frisbie (Harvest House Publishers, 2006).

My Single Mom Life: Stories and Practical Lessons for Your Journey, by Angela Thomas (Thomas Nelson, 2008).

Parenting with Love and Logic, by Foster Cline and Jim Fay (Pinon Press, 2006).

Pictures Your Heart Remembers: Building Lasting Memories of Love & Acceptance in Your Family, by John Trent (WaterBrook Press, 2000).

Raising a Modern-Day Knight: A Father's Role in Guiding His Son to Authentic Manhood, by Robert Lewis (Tyndale House, 2007).

Raising Girls, by Melissa Trevathan & Sissy Goff (Zondervan, 2007).

Second Chances: Men, Women and Children a Decade After Divorce, by Judith Wallerstein, Julia Lewis, and Sandra Blakeslee (Houghton Mifflin, 1996).

She Calls Me Daddy, by Robert Wolgemuth and Gary Smalley (Tyndale House, 1999).

She Still Calls Me Daddy: Building a New Relationship with Your Daughter After You Walk Her Down the Aisle, by Robert Wolgemuth (Thomas Nelson, 2009).

The Backdoor to Your Teen's Heart, by Melissa Trevathan & Sissy Goff (Harvest House, 2002).

The Christian Family Guide to Surviving Divorce, by Pamela Weintraub and Steven R. R. Clark (Alpha, 2003).

The Five Love Languages of Children, by Gary Chapman and Ross Campbell, MD (Northfield, 1997).

The Good Divorce: Keeping Your Family Together When Your Marriage Comes Apart, by Constance Ahrons, PhD (Harper Perennial, 1994).

The Long-Distance Dad: How You Can Be There for Your Child – Whether Divorced, Deployed, or on the Road, by Steven Ashley (Adams Media, 2008).

The Power of a Praying Parent, by Stormie Omartian (Harvest House, 2007).

The Single Dad's Survival Guide, by Mike Klumpp (Waterbrook, 2003).

The Stepfamily Survival Guide, by Natalie Nichols Gillespie (Revell, 2004).

The Smart Stepfamily: Seven Steps to a Healthy Family, by Ron L. Deal (Bethany House, 2002).

The Smart Stepmom: Practical Steps to Help You THRIVE! by Ron L. Deal and Laura Petherbridge (Bethany House, 2009).

The Unexpected Legacy of Divorce: A 25 Year Landmark Study, by Judith Wallerstein, Julia Lewis, and Sandra Blakeslee (Hyperion, 2000).

They Call Me Dad, by Ken Canfield (Howard Books, 2005).

When "I Do" Becomes "I Don't": Practical Steps for Healing During Separation and Divorce, by Laura Petherbridge (David C. Cook, 2008).

When the One You Love Wants to Leave, by Donald R. Harvey (Revell, 2005).

When the Vow Breaks: A Survival and Recovery Guide for Christians Facing Divorce, by Joseph Warren Kniskern and Steve Grissom (B&H Books, 2008).

When Your Marriage Dies: Answers to Questions About Separation and Divorce, by Laura Petherbridge (David C. Cook, 2005).

Books on Sex Education for Children
by Stan and Brenna Jones

All published by Navpress, 2007:

The Story of Me (ages 3-5)

Before I Was Born (ages 5-8)

What's the Big Deal: Why God Cares About Sex (ages 8-11)

Facing the Facts (ages 11-14)

How and When to Tell Your Kids About Sex (parents' resource)

Books by/for Adult Children of Divorce

Adult Children of Divorced Parents: Making Your Marriage Work, by Beverly and Tom Rodgers (Resources Publications, 2002).

Between Two Worlds: The Inner Lives of Children of Divorce, by Elizabeth Marquardt (Crown, 2005).

Breaking the Cycle of Divorce, by Dr. John Trent (Tyndale, 2006).

The Love They Lost: Living with the Legacy of Our Parents' Divorce, by Stephanie Staal (Delacorte Press, 2000).

Father Fiction: Chapters for a Fatherless Generation, by Don Miller (Howard Books, 2010).

Split: Stories from a Generation Raised on Divorce, by Ava Chin, editor (Contemporary Books, 2002).

Using Children's Books
to Help Your Children Cope
with Family Change

Researchers Harvey and Fine (2004) tell us that, in order to activate children's resilient mechanisms, we should "highlight the value of storytelling and giving voice to young children about the pain of divorce and to their special odysseys of adaptation to these divorce-related losses in their families." Because they lack the emotional vocabulary to describe or understand what they are experiencing, children often find it difficult to express their emotions or their needs when their family splits. But this difficult task is sometimes made easier for them if they can distance themselves through vicarious experiences in books or films. For very young children, picture books that use animals or toys as characters are particularly helpful, allowing the children to vent feelings or emotions in a nonthreatening way. Books like this can help ease the psychological burden children feel as a result of their parental divorce.

I suggest that, after discussing this with your co-parent, the two of you select several of the children's books I suggest below — or others you find that meet your children's needs or appeal to their particular interests. Buy *two* copies: one for Mom's house and one for Dad's. Not only does that ensure that the book is available to the child when she needs it; it also reinforces the idea that Mom and Dad are in communication and working together for the child's welfare.

As The Crow Flies, by Elizabeth Mahoney Winthrop (Clarion Books, 1998).

Dinosaurs Divorce, by Mark Brown and Laurie Krasny (Little, Brown Books for Young Readers, 1988).

I Don't Want to Talk About It, by Jeanie Franz Ransom (Magination Press, 2000).

I Live With Daddy, by Judith Vigna (Albert Whitman and Company, 1997).

It's Not Your Fault KoKo Bear, Vicki Lansky (Book Peddlers, 1997).

Loon Summer, by Barbara Santucci (Eerdmans Books for Young Readers, 2010).

Mama and Daddy Bear's Divorce, by Cornelia Maude Spelman and Kathy Parkinson (Albert Whitman and Company, 1998).

Missing Rabbit, by Roni Schotter (Clarion Books, 2002).

Room for Rabbit, by Roni Schotter (Clarion Books, 2003).

What Children Need to Know When Parents Get Divorced, by William L. Coleman (Bethany House, 1998).

When Mom and Dad Separate: Children Can Learn to Cope with Grief from Divorce, by Marge Heegaard (Woodland Press, 1990).

Notes

1. Mavis Hetherington, "The Virginia Longitudinal Study of Divorce and Remarriage."

2. N. Chase, ed., "An overview of theory, research, and societal issues," *Burdened Children* (New York: Guilford, 1999), 3–33.

3. S. Minuchin, B. Montalvo, B. Guerney, B. Rosman, and F. Schumer, *Families of the Slums* (New York: Basic Books, 1967).

4. Samuel López de Victoria, PhD, *Harming Your Child by Making Him Your Parent* (Psych Central, 2010). Psych Central has been noted in the *New York Times*, the *Wall Street Journal*, the *Los Angeles Times*, *Newsweek*, *TIME*, *U.S. News & World Report*, the *Washington Post*, *USA Today*, *USA Weekend*, *The Village Voice*, *Business Week*, *Forbes* magazine, and dozens of other publications.

5. P. R. Amato and B. Keith, "Parental divorce and the well-being of children: A meta-analysis," *Psychological Bulletin* 110 (1991), 26–46.

6. S. M. Green, E. R. Anderson, E. R. Hetherington, M. S. Forgatch and D. S. DeGarmo, "Risk and resilience after divorce," in *Normal family processes: Growing diversity and complexity*, ed. F. Walsh, 3rd ed. (New York: Guilford, 2003), 96–120.

7. P. R. Amato, "Children's adjustment to divorce: Theories, hypotheses, and empirical support," *Journal of Marriage and the Family* 55 (1993): 23–38 and Joan B. Kelly and Robert E. Emery, "Children's adjustment following divorce: Risk and resilience perspectives," *Family Relations* 52, no. 4 (October 2003): 352–62.

8. Isolina Ricci, PhD, *Mom's House, Dad's House: Making Two Homes for Your Child* (New York: Simon & Schuster, 1997).

9. Kelly and Emery, "Children's adjustment following divorce," 352.

10. Ibid.

11. Ibid.

12. Ibid.

13. National Fatherhood Initiative, *Father Facts*, 5th ed. (2007).

14. J. Dunn, L. Davies, T. O'Connor, and W. Sturgess, "Family lives and friendships: The perspectives of children in step-, single-parent, and nonstep families," *Journal of Family Psychology* 15 (2001): 272–87.

15. J. Wallerstein and J. Kelly, "California's children of divorce," *Psychology Today* (1980): 67–76.

16. C. Ahrons, *The Good Divorce* (New York: HarperCollins, 1994).

17. M. Hetherington and J. Kelly, *For Better or For Worse: Divorce Reconsidered* (New York: Norton, 2002).

18. Kelly and Emery, "Children's adjustment following divorce," 352.

19. R. Deal and L. Petherbridge, *The Smart Stepmom: Practical Steps to Help You Thrive* (Bloomington, Minn.: Bethany House, 2009).

20. R. Deal, *The Smart Stepdad* (Bloomington, Minn.: Bethany House, 2011).

21. J. Trent, *Breaking the Cycle of Divorce: How Your Marriage Can Succeed Even if Your Parents' Didn't* (Carol Stream, Ill.: Tyndale, 2006).

Continue your co-parenting journey with Co-Parenting International!

We offer:

- Additional online resources
- DVD and audio products
- Free monthly e-newsletter
- Free article downloads
- Webinar events to help build co-parenting skills
- Local and national organization links
- Required co-parenting classes available for divorcing parents
- Small group curriculum video segments by Tammy Daughtry, The Co-Parenting Coach

Don't forget to submit questions to be addressed in articles and e-newsletters, and attend a live seminar or conference.

Visit *www.coparentinginternational.com*
to learn to be the co-parent your child deserves.

Co-Parenting International
Working Together to Help Your Children Thrive

Discover More Online

Enjoy free videos as Tammy Daughtry introduces each of the book sections at *www.CoparentingInternational.com*.

Learn more about *Co-Parenting Works!* with eight new videos that delve into the topics of the book.

Share Your Thoughts

With the Author: Your comments will be forwarded to the author when you send them to *zauthor@zondervan.com*.

With Zondervan: Submit your review of this book by writing to *zreview@zondervan.com*.

Free Online Resources at
www.zondervan.com

Daily Bible Verses and Devotions: Enrich your life with daily Bible verses or devotions that help you start every morning focused on God. Visit www.zondervan.com/newsletters.

Free Email Publications: Sign up for newsletters on Christian living, academic resources, church ministry, fiction, children's resources, and more. Visit www.zondervan.com/newsletters.

Zondervan Bible Search: Find and compare Bible passages in a variety of translations at www.zondervanbiblesearch.com.

Other Benefits: Register to receive online benefits like coupons and special offers, or to participate in research.